Corporate Strategy

Book 11
International Strategy

Book 12
The Dynamics of Strategy

MBA
Strategy

The Open University

BUSINESS SCHOOL

The Open University,
Walton Hall, Milton Keynes MK7 6AA

First published 1996. Second edition 1998. Reprinted 1999

Copyright © 1998 The Open University

All rights reserved. No part of this work may be reproduced, stored in a retrieval system or transmitted, in any form or by any means, without written permission from the publisher or a licence from the Copyright Licensing Agency Ltd. Details of such licences (for reprographic reproduction) may be obtained from the Copyright Licensing Agency Ltd, 90 Tottenham Court Road, London W1P 0LP.

Edited, designed and typeset by The Open University

Printed in the United Kingdom by Henry Ling Limited, The Dorset Press, Dorchester, Dorset DT1 1HD

ISBN 0 7492 9210 5

Further information on Open University Business School courses may be obtained from the Course Sales Development Centre, The Open University, PO Box 222, Milton Keynes MK7 6YY (Telephone: 01908 653449).

oubs.open.ac.uk

2.2

BOOK 10

Corporate Strategy

Author: Eric Cassells

MBA

Strategy

Contents

1	**Introduction**	**5**
	1.1 Learning objectives of this book	5
2	**Strategies for the corporation**	**7**
	2.1 Corporate strategy and portfolio combinations	10
	2.2 Synergy in corporations	14
	2.3 Strategic capabilities and corporate strategy	20
3	**Diversification and divestment**	**25**
	3.1 Diversification strategies	25
	3.2 Divestment	27
4	**Strategies for corporate structure**	**32**
	4.1 The structures of corporations	32
	4.2 Alternative influences on corporate strategy and structure	33
	4.3 Tools for the strategy manager	40
5	**Networks and corporations**	**45**
	5.1 Networks and institutional frameworks	45
	5.2 The distinctiveness of networks	48
6	**Summary and conclusion**	**52**
	References	**53**
	Acknowledgements	**55**

1 INTRODUCTION

This book examines corporate strategy and its relationship to business strategy. Book 1 identified the relationship of corporate and business strategy through the convention of a hierarchical diagram (see Figure 1.1). Corporate strategy is the overarching strategy that applies to a number of businesses combined within a single corporation. Corporate strategy is multibusiness strategy.

Multibusiness strategy means more, however, than simply aggregating the strategies of a number of businesses. Mere scale, size or variety of businesses does not guarantee superior performance for a corporation. These factors may not even cover the extra costs of running a number of activities as a corporation rather than as separate businesses. There must be identifiable benefits from combining separate businesses together in a single corporation to make corporate strategy worthwhile.

Corporate strategy is therefore concerned with achieving superior returns, not because of superior performance within the separate businesses themselves, but through their *combination*. It is not concerned with simply growing the returns of a single business – that is the province of business strategy. Corporate strategy may, however, be concerned with increasing or reducing the number and variety of businesses in the corporation, so as to create a more effective combination. As a consequence, diversifying activities, either by acquisition or internal development, or divesting existing activities, are important elements in corporate strategy.

In this book, therefore, our primary focus will be on identifying strategies and tools which help corporations obtain superior returns from the combination of their activities. Section 2 of the book concentrates on this area. In Section 3 we discuss decision criteria and alternative strategies for diversification and divestment. Section 4 deals with the methods and techniques developed by corporate managers over the years to help them manage the corporation's combination of businesses more effectively. Section 5, taking account of the fact that these tools are predominantly based on the experience of US and UK corporations, examines some of the alternative combination benefits which are available from corporate forms, such as networks, more readily found in other countries.

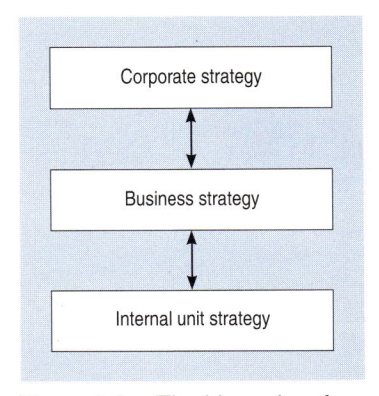

Figure 1.1 The hierarchy of levels of strategy in an organisation

1.1 LEARNING OBJECTIVES OF THIS BOOK

After studying this book you should be able to:
- evaluate the main approaches to corporate strategy, and their likely contribution to superior performance for a corporation
- develop a framework for evaluating the attractiveness of diversification and divestment strategies
- demonstrate the way that fashions and the availability of management tools have influenced the theory and practice of corporate strategy, structure and management

- demonstrate the role of institutional, cultural, regulatory and socio-economic environments in shaping corporations around the world
- assess the increasing significance of collaboration and core competencies in our understanding of how distinctive corporate benefits can be achieved from combining business activities.

2 Strategies for the corporation

The following mini-case contains a number of examples of how one major European corporation has attempted to gain superior performance by realising corporate strategy benefits from combining some of the activities of four distinct businesses in the 1990s.

MINI-CASE: FOUR WHEELS ON THE 'PEOPLE'S WAGEN'

The Volkswagen Group of companies was one of Europe's top three car manufacturers in 1996. The VW group included the VW, Audi, SEAT and Skoda brands. Of these, VW brand volume sales were most significant to the group. Audi produced cars for the executive segments. SEAT and Skoda had strong positions in their domestic Spanish and Czech markets, respectively, but were also focused on the economy and compact car segments in other European markets.

Audi

Audi had a strong reputation for the engineering and build quality of their German-built cars. Audis sold well, but the dynamic and interior specifications of the Audi 80 and 100 had been regarded as inferior to class leaders such as BMW and Mercedes.

This changed, however, with the 1995 introduction of the Audi A6 and A4. The latter was commonly regarded as at least as effective as the BMW 3 series, and improved Audi's market penetration in the key entry level of the executive segments. The following year Audi launched a new product line with the compact A3, in an emerging segment in the executive market. This launch marked a completely revitalised Audi product line.

SEAT

SEAT was acquired by VW, after a failed joint venture with Fiat. The SEAT brands sold well in Spain, but commanded only a small market share in the rest of Europe. VW's engineering reputation had gradually improved the reputation of SEAT cars. SEAT models were priced, however, to appeal to price-sensitive buyers. VW believed that cheaper Spanish labour and a separate identity could provide a channel for rebadging products for economy buyers, without damaging its own mid-market reputation.

SEAT was a costly investment, however. Labour unrest, inefficient manufacturing and spiralling costs led to losses of $1.1 billion and $150 million in 1993 and 1994, respectively. A $1.9 billion investment in a new factory, opened in 1992, experienced ongoing problems. Worse, this investment had been financed with Deutschmarks, repayments were paid from peseta revenues, the loans were unhedged, and the peseta devalued by 30 per cent relative to the mark between 1992 and 1996.

Skoda

Czechoslovak manufacturer Skoda had been the source of a rich tradition of jokes amongst Western car owners prior to VW's acquisition. VW set about introducing VW-derived models to replace old Skoda models, and Skoda's reputation improved when VW engineering practices were introduced to the

Czech factories. As in Spain, cheap skilled labour was an attraction. Skoda models were also intended to appeal to the new price-sensitive consumers of Eastern Europe.

By 1996, however, Skoda's sales in the small Czech and Slovak markets were falling as western cars penetrated these previously closed markets. Large sales in Eastern European markets had not materialised, and Skoda's penetration of the Western European budget segments had not been significant.

The VW brand

The European volume car market served by VW was oversupplied, and costly battles for market share drove down margins. Japanese manufacturers had taken significant market share competing on efficient high-reliability global-scale manufacturing, and establishing production within the European Union to overcome restrictions on imports. The traditional Europe-based manufacturers had responded by improving productivity, efficiency and product quality, and by cutting employment.

VW had, however, been slower to respond to the challenges. It had recorded losses in 1993, returning to profitability in 1994, but margins for 1996 were expected to be only 1 per cent of sales. This compared to, for example, Fiat (over 3 per cent) and General Motors (6 per cent). In addition, VW had some unique problems:

- The European market was the slowest growing but most competitive of the major automobile markets. VW depended on this market for 75 per cent of its sales.
- VW's few overseas operations had uneven prospects. While Brazil was booming, dominant positions in China and Mexico were seriously threatened.
- VW was heavily dependent on cars produced in Germany, with its high labour costs and strong currency. While 42 per cent of the workforce were based in Germany, they accounted for 58 per cent of all payroll charges.
- Higher costs were driving VW's prices higher. For example, while VW had shared the development costs of the Sharan people-carrier with Ford, the Ford Galaxy was selling for over $1,000 less.
- VW's engineering quality had, it was estimated, allowed it to charge a price premium of between 5 per cent and 10 per cent. Surveys by J. D. Power in 1995 indicated, however, that driver perceptions were changing, finding VW only average in terms of mechanical reliability.

Productivity at VW in 1994 amounted to 12 vehicles per worker. This compared poorly with European competitors: Fiat produced 16 vehicles per worker, Opel 19, and Ford 20. It was estimated that 30,000 VW German workers were underemployed. New models only threatened to increase underemployment; the 1995 Polo could be assembled in 36 per cent less time than its predecessor. The government of Lower Saxony, however, owned a 20 per cent block of VW shares, and was reluctant to allow VW to reduce its workforce.

Natural wastage might account for approximately 6,000 jobs each year, but VW had been forced to cut labour costs in other ways:

- Weekly hours for the German labour force had been cut by 21 per cent in 1994. This resulted in a 16 per cent saving in labour costs, but the 5 per cent differential had added a further $1.5 billion to the accounted unit costs of VW cars.

- José Ignacio Lopez de Arriotura was controversially recruited from General Motors to reduce supply costs. VW broke existing supply contracts, and forced suppliers to bid anew for contracts. Lopez's supplier strategy was partly reversed, however, when manufacture of some supplies was in-sourced to reduce the underemployment of VW's expensive labour force. This in-sourcing saw VW manufacturing car door trims, a practice unheard of at other car manufacturers.

Volkswagen group strategies

The acquisition of SEAT and Skoda had marginally diversified Volkswagen's dependency on north western European markets. Spain, the Czech Republic, and Slovakia also offered cheaper skilled labour, and SEAT and Skoda learned from VW's engineering and build expertise.

Further, VW had a strong position in European mid-market volume cars, Audi in executive cars, with SEAT and Skoda branded for the economy market segments. Given the scale available from combining these operation, Volkswagen saw the chance of reducing costs by standardising parts and assemblies for a number of final products. The group planned, for example, to offer two types of horn on all models, replacing 46 variants.

In addition to reducing the variety of parts across the group, a reduction in the number of car platforms from 16 to 4 was planned: previously all four companies would design and build separate floorpans, suspension systems and engine mountings. The first result of this was the 1995 VW Polo, matched with SEAT and Skoda models. A new VW Golf compact was planned for 1997, using the same platform as the Audio A3, with SEAT and Skoda models to follow. In the same way, the 1996 VW Passat used the Audi A4 platform. This policy would, it was hoped, improve group profits by over $500 million annually, a saving of $150 per car.

(Adapted from International Business Week, *26 February 1996)*

Activity 2.1

Earlier we stated that corporate strategy was concerned with superior performance that resulted from combining separate businesses. Using the mini-case, identify the benefits that Volkswagen hopes to derive from combining the four car companies within one corporation. Secondly, identify any examples in the mini-case where combining separate activities has been less successful for the corporation.

Discussion

The four car companies have very distinct identities. The following main benefits may be available from their combination as one corporation:

1 *The companies span the complete range of market segments, allowing the corporation to build a portfolio of distinct brand assets.*

2 *There is geographic complementarity between the strength of the VW and Audi brands in north and west Europe, that of SEAT in Spain, and Skoda in the Czech Republic and Slovakia.*

3 *Corporations gain benefits from locating different activities in different countries, according to the relative input costs. Expensive German labour made costs a problem, but the*

relatively cheap labour of SEAT and Skoda allows the corporation to price economy models competitively.

4 *The strategy of sharing common parts, assemblies and designed components has the potential to save the corporation $500 million each year.*

There are, however, two main areas where the combination of separate activities does not seem so successful:

1 *The political pressures on the VW brand have led to in-sourcing activities which conventional wisdom suggests are better handled by specialist suppliers.*

2 *The cross-currency investment arrangement for the SEAT manufacturing plant led to significant exchange loses. Unhedged currency financing seems an inappropriate activity to combine with a core business of manufacturing cars.*

We will return to the VW mini-case later. While there are considerable potential benefits from VW's corporate strategy, the mini-case does not cover the extent to which its competitors are pursuing similar or superior corporate strategies. The reality is, of course, that manufacturers such as General Motors, Toyota and Ford are also gaining benefits from the standardisation of design, parts and assembly manufacture, and the use of international locations to reduce the costs of inputs. VW are, therefore, in a competitive process where ideas of how best to combine separate businesses are themselves part of competition; VW's $500 million cost savings from standardisation will not provide any *advantage* if Ford or Toyota save the same amount or more from similar programmes.

The history of the last forty years in corporate strategy is one where ideas about the most effective way to benefit from combining separate activities have changed as corporations have sought to outperform each other. The first of these ideas we will examine is 'portfolio management'.

2.1 CORPORATE STRATEGY AND PORTFOLIO COMBINATIONS

The view that corporate strategy benefits can be obtained by combining a portfolio of diversified strategic business units was immensely popular during the 1970s and 1980s. It was the orthodox way to manage corporations during this period.

2.1.1 The development of portfolio management in corporate strategy

You may have already encountered portfolio techniques in earlier studies.

You should now refresh your knowledge and understanding by reading the Set Book section entitled 'Managing the corporate portfolio', from page 393 to the end of the sub-section 'Portfolio planning models: BCG's growth-share matrix' on page 398.

Grant gives a good summary of the uses of portfolio analyses. As corporate tools for adding value to businesses they can be useful in allocating resources, giving direction to business units, setting performance targets, and for the combination benefits of portfolios. Grant suggests that the main benefits of portfolios to corporations are the synergies that come from using internal cash flows to finance the corporation, and planning for the replacement of declining businesses with growing ones.

2.1.2 The relationship of portfolio management to industry attractiveness and superior resources

Portfolio management has strong links to the views of Michael Porter (1980) that superior profitability derives from the structure of attractive industries, as discussed in Books 3 and 5. It also captures something of the view that superior profitability comes from a superior resource position relative to competitors: both the BCG and GE/McKinsey matrices position businesses according to industry attractiveness and their relative competitive position in an industry.

As you saw in the Set Book, BCG produced a framework on two axes: relative market share and market growth rate. The matrix builds on two underlying concepts, the experience curve and the product life-cycle. (If you need further explanation of these two concepts, please refer to pages 196–8 and 242–6 respectively in the Set Book.):

- Relative market share indicates a business's market power (one potential source of competitive advantage), and this is equated with its ability to earn above average rates of return. In the extreme, higher returns derive from a monopoly – that is, exploiting a 100 per cent market share. More often, however, having a large market share will coincide with cost benefits from large production runs (economies of scale) and from large cumulative volumes of production (experience curve benefits).

- The importance of high market growth in the BCG matrix is related to the product life-cycle concept, which suggests that growth will be minimal or negative when a product is mature. The life-cycle and experience curve can interact in a virtuous circle, however, if a product achieves a dominant position in a market during its growth, achieving early benefits from the experience curve, and ultimately building market share to exploit economies of scale.

The BCG Growth-Share Matrix therefore implies that businesses with market power in a growing market ('stars') will, with proper investment, mature to become 'cash cows', generating significant amounts of net cash. A corporation can therefore secure its future by combining a balanced portfolio of stars and cash cows, the latter to fund the former as they grow. This is the core notion that led to the matrix's popularity for managing diversified corporations.

Activity 2.2

Over the years since the BCG growth-share matrix was developed there have been a number of criticisms of it. Its two-dimensional nature is probably its fundamental weakness. From your earlier studies on this course, list other variables which you consider significant in determining industry attractiveness and the competitive position of a business.

Discussion

It is not that relative market share and market growth rates are unimportant, rather that there is a host of other relevant variables. For example, growth and position in a market life-cycle may be important, but they do not take account of the threat of new entrants, substitutes, and the power of customers and suppliers which Porter (1980) identified in his 'five forces' analysis of industry structure (Book 3). In the same way, although the BCG matrix describes superior resources in terms of experience curve benefits and market power, it cannot capture the sources of advantage found in the whole range of distinctive resources and capabilities discussed in Books 4 and 5.

2.1.3 Questioning portfolio management

> Coca-Cola Co. discovered that it had inadvertently bought Columbia Pictures Inc. Company executives had thought they were buying Colombia, the Central American country. Coca-Cola is asking the movie company for its deposit back.
>
> (Off The Wall Street Journal, *1982*)

Portfolio management as the accepted means of managing corporate strategy coincided with the growth of diversified conglomerates in the 1970s. Often these conglomerates consisted of portfolios of unrelated businesses, where the management of corporate cash flows between the businesses was the sole underlying rationale. This period was accompanied by a pattern of acquisitions of unrelated businesses, often followed by the divestment or liquidation of those classified as 'dogs', and deemed to be of no further use in generating cash for the corporation. The quote which introduced this section satirises the recklessness of some of the acquisitions made at the time.

The late 1980s, however, saw a move away from ready acceptance of portfolios as the best means of managing corporate strategy. This was partly the result of the perception (supported by empirical research findings such as Grant *et al.*, 1988) that the performance of many diversified corporations pursuing portfolio strategies had deteriorated, as their management capabilities became overstretched. This may be a function of diversity, sheer size, or the difficulties experienced in processing and interpreting corporate information.

There has since been a tendency for corporations to talk instead of their 'focus' on 'core businesses', reflecting a need to simplify their strategies. Remember the example of BOC Industrial Gases in Book 5. BOC IG diversified its portfolio to acquire companies that *use* gas, only to divest these later and refocus on its original industrial gas *supply* business. More recently, after Swiss pharmaceutical companies Sandoz and Ciba were merged to form Novartis in 1995, it decided to demerge and divest Ciba's Speciality Chemicals business and concentrate on the pharmaceuticals businesses which were at the heart of its activities.

2.1.4 Shareholder portfolios, not corporate portfolios

The main theoretical criticisms of portfolio strategies have come from the fields of finance and economics. The benefits of financial portfolios were first evaluated in the 1950s (Markowitz, 1952). By acquiring a portfolio of shares with different patterns of dividend payments and capital appreciation, a shareholder reduces the risk that attaches to any one stock. Portfolio theory further provides a means of distinguishing a share's risk between market risk and unique, diversifiable risk; that is, between the risk of holding a portfolio of stocks which replicates the composition of the entire stock market, and risk that is specific to an individual stock. The parallels between financial portfolio theory and the corporate strategy portfolio models of BCG and McKinsey are obvious. In trying to balance stars and cash cows the corporate strategy manager acts like the shareholder, reducing the unique risk that comes from owning one business.

The manager of the diversified corporation is *not*, however, a shareholder investing in a portfolio of stocks in the market. Portfolio theory is based on the assumption of perfect markets, and a perfect market is dependent on the availability of perfect information. Critics of corporate portfolios submit, however, that in a perfect market it is the task of shareholders to use that information to construct a portfolio according to their own risk/return profiles. In a perfect market it is unclear how a corporate portfolio manager can add further value for shareholders. Indeed, diversified corporations submerge information about individual businesses in less informative corporate reports, and add the transaction costs (as discussed in Books 4 and 8) of managing corporate portfolios to the costs which a shareholder has to bear.

Supporters of the perfect market question, therefore, whether it is shareholders or managers who benefit from corporate portfolios. Jensen and Meckling (1976), for example, argue that managers have an interest in diversifying the corporate portfolio to reduce the risk of bankruptcy, increase their job security and increase the size of the corporation (and, with it, their salaries and personal power). In particular, the retention of excess cash to fund the development of 'stars' is one of the ways in which managers 'avoid monitoring by the financial markets and ... invest in expansion, diversification, and organisational slack which yields below market returns' (Gibbs, 1993). In agency theory (as suggested in Book 2), corporate portfolio diversification by management is often bad for shareholders.

Activity 2.3

How can we explain fashion in corporate strategy techniques, as evidenced by the rise and fall in the popularity of portfolio management?

Discussion

Portfolio management was pioneered by General Electric (GE), Boston Consulting Group (BCG), and McKinsey, three widely admired organisations. Their techniques and experience were reported in the business press. The experience of GE, one of the most widely diversified conglomerates, was particularly influential in validating the technique. The role of GE in legitimising portfolio strategies was akin to the role that General Motors played in validating the use of the divisionalised form to manage diverse corporate activities. Whereas the experiences of General Motors helped to define the corporate strategist's role in controlling divisional resource allocation and output performance, GE's portfolio management extended that role to balancing the portfolio of corporate activities. Portfolio balancing and diversification required the corporate strategist to acquire and divest business units.

Thinking about strategy occurs within its own institutional and ideological framework (Rumelt et al., 1994). In the 1950s and 1960s, business schools such as Harvard played an important role in developing models and frameworks to help strategists. The 1970s and 1980s, however, saw the rise of consulting practices as a source of new thinking about strategy. BCG became the world's largest strategy consulting firm. Later, Michael Porter at Harvard was important in setting an agenda for thinking about strategy that predominated in the 1980s. Porter (1980) emphasised the study of industry attractiveness – echoing and validating one of the main strategic variables in portfolio management.

The declining popularity of portfolio management in the late 1980s and 1990s can be considered in the same way. Despite continuing to use portfolio techniques in the 1980s, GE's CEO Jack Welch sought greater clarity and simplicity for their corporate structure by identifying three mainstream business activities. Welch once again allowed his new ideas to be reported in an influential profile in Forbes *magazine. Secondly, in the 1990s, the agenda for thinking about strategy began to move away from industry attractiveness towards distinctive resources and capabilities as a source of superior performance. With the exception of its focus on experience curve benefits, portfolio analysis did not resonate well with this new strategy paradigm.*

Anglo-American ideas of the pre-eminence of shareholder interests in corporate strategy management have also led to an increasing focus on shareholder value analysis techniques as a tool for managing diversified businesses. You should now read the sub-section in the Set Book entitled 'Value-based approaches to corporate restructuring' on pages 398–400.

2.2 SYNERGY IN CORPORATIONS

Grant suggests that the benefits of portfolio strategies are the *synergies* that come from using internal cash flows to finance the corporation. Synergy is often put forward as the justification for acquiring or merging two separate businesses. The familiar explanation of synergy is the effect by which 'the whole exceeds the sum of the parts'. The 'equation' 2 + 2 = 5 is often used to demonstrate this effect.

Such statements have proven seductive to managers. Their simplicity belies the complexity of achieving the proposed benefits. A senior director at the UK drinks and confectionery group Cadbury-Schweppes described the initial five years after the merger of Cadbury's confectionery and Schweppes' soft drinks businesses as one where corporate management 'waited, as if for Godot, for the synergy'. The mere act of positioning businesses within the same portfolio does not add value. Synergy needs to be created.

2.2.1 Synergy and negative synergy

Synergy describes a corporation's ability to create value, by identifying the fit between the opportunities arising from *combining activities* and the corporation's capabilities in exploiting these opportunities. Not all corporations will seek to exploit all available synergies, however. Some diversified conglomerates may only look for financial synergies. The UK conglomerate Hanson had little apparent interest in attempts to benefit from combining subsidiaries' activities; its main source of success stemmed from centrally imposing the 'financial control' of its corporate headquarters upon its separate subsidiaries.

Managers should also be alert to the dangers of *negative synergy* – the potential disadvantages and costs of a poor combination. In an inappropriate or badly handled diversification, value can be destroyed, rather than created. In these instances, the negative synergy effect can be described as 'the sum of the parts being greater than the whole', or 2 + 2 = 3.

Many conglomerates in the late 1980s and early 1990s have been devalued by investors to reflect such negative synergy. Indeed, Hanson had a successful strategy of acquiring UK and US quoted corporations where the value of the separate businesses exceeded the value of the corporation. Imperial Group, Smith Corona Machines (SCM) and Kidde Fire were all bought at prices considerably lower than the sum of values that Hanson later realised from their parts, either by running them more effectively or by selling businesses to outsiders who could. The most spectacular example of this strategy remains the acquisition in 1989 of SCM by Hanson for $1.3 billion. Having quickly recouped the purchase price by selling a number of SCM businesses for $1.5 billion, Hanson was left with SCM's core electronic typewriter business with a value subsequently estimated at $2 billion.

By contrast, some of the difficulties of achieving 'obvious' potential synergies are illustrated in the Anheuser-Busch mini-case which follows.

MINI-CASE: THE SYNERGY MIRAGE – ANHEUSER-BUSCH

Anheuser-Busch is the largest brewing company in the US, with dominant brands, Budweiser and Bud Light, in the two key segments of the beer market. It fought a long battle in the 1970s for dominance in the US beer market with its main rival Miller. It recorded a 44 per cent market share in 1995. Early 1996 was to see Anheuser finally admit defeat, however, on a strategy to gain synergies from building businesses that would complement its beer core.

1979 was a good year for Anheuser; having fought off Miller's market share wars, it could use the cash flowing from buoyant demand in the beer market to fund other activities. Anheuser decided, therefore, to start a complementary business in snack foods. Three years later, this strategy was extended to the bread business through the $560 million acquisition of Campbell Taggart bakeries.

The synergies appeared well thought out. Anheuser's strengths were its marketing and logistics skills. Those marketing skills were planned to allow Anheuser to build up its new Eagle Snacks subsidiary to challenge PepsiCo's Frito Lay subsidiary, and to create national brands for Campbell Taggart in the fragmented bread market. Anheuser's beer distributors would deliver Eagle's snack foods to bars, inns, and supermarkets, and Campbell Taggart's bread to supermarkets, at the same time as they made their beer deliveries. Finally, Anheuser's beer and bread businesses could allow economies of scale in buying yeast, a main input to both products.

The synergies did not, however, emerge in practice:

- Beer distributors saw bread and snacks as a diversion from their core business, and were less than enthusiastic about the strategy.
- Selling the products to supermarkets and convenience retail outlets was more complicated than Anheuser's planners predicted: bread, beer and snacks were displayed in different areas of the stores and involved selling to different purchasing officers.

> - A patchwork of distributors emerged selling beer only, snacks only, bread only, two of the products, or all three, thus creating managerial complexity in Anheuser's logistics operations.
> - Frito Lay responded with vigour to Eagle Snacks' innovations, discouraging distributors from carrying a snack sideline in competition against a strong market leader (Frito Lay held between 40 and 50 per cent of the market throughout, as against Eagle Snacks' 4 to 6 per cent).
> - Campbell Taggart was unable to establish a national brand in breads, due to the growth of supermarkets' own 'private-label' brands.
>
> In late 1995, Eagle Snacks announced a $25 million loss on revenues of $400 million, and Anheuser finally admitted defeat after seventeen consecutive years of losses. After discussing a sale with eight possible buyers, Anheuser was forced to announce the complete closure of Eagle in early 1996. No buyer was willing to invest the estimated $250 million required to build viable market share and make Eagle Snacks profitable. Campbell Taggart was only marginally profitable with net revenues of $50 million on sales of $1.5 billion in 1995. The synergies between bread and beer had never been truly realised, and Anheuser announced the demerger of Campbell-Taggart in 1995.
>
> (Adapted from International Business Week, 4 March 1996)

The Anheuser mini-case demonstrates the difficulties corporations encounter in identifying and realising the benefits of synergy.

At face value, Anheuser had identified potential benefits of combining beer, snacks and bread businesses. The realisation of such synergies, however, was embedded in a number of seemingly quite routine tasks, such as selling all products to single purchasing officers in retail stores, and persuading beer distributors that they could benefit from delivering all three product lines. The capabilities required to allow the synergies to be realised were not controlled by Anheuser.

There were also negative synergies, such as the diversion of funds from the more profitable beer business and the increased complication of the management task of Anheuser's logistics business.

2.2.2 Synergy and the nature of assets

The deliberate combination of assets, resources and capabilities from separate businesses is a distinguishing feature of corporate strategy. Itami (1992) draws a distinction between 'physical' and 'invisible' assets, and the type of combination benefits which originate from each.

'Complementary' benefits can be obtained from the simple combination of physical assets, such as factories and machinery. These can be achieved when physical assets are underutilised, incapable of being fully utilised (for example, due to seasonal cycles), or because combining them reduces uncertainty or risk (for example, in portfolio strategies). Such benefits may include economies of scale, higher capacity utilisation, improved cash flow and improved product line and mix. Itami quotes the example of bulk carrier vessels, which carry Japanese cars to the US West Coast, loading up with timber from Washington and Oregon in an unrelated trade returning to Japan.

> Permitting two unrelated strategy elements to coexist, usually through the utilisation of the same physical or financial assets, is the essence of the complement effect.
>
> (Itami, 1992, p. 43)

Invisible assets such as corporate culture, technical expertise, a strong corporate or brand image, or expert knowledge of the marketplace, may be transferred from one business to another. This combination benefit is described by Itami as the 'synergy effect'. The Japanese condiments company Ajinomoto, for example, has used its strong brand image to sell products such as salad oil, mayonnaise, and bouillon cubes. Ajinomoto's second synergy benefit has come from spreading its knowledge in amino acid technology into pharmaceuticals manufacturing.

> The essence of invisible assets is information.... Information has three characteristics that make synergy possible: it can be used simultaneously, it does not wear out from overuse, and bits of it can be combined to yield even more information.
>
> (Itami, p. 45)

Itami establishes a narrower definition of the term synergy than is commonly used in strategy (or that we implied in Section 2.2.1). His distinction between complementary and synergy combination benefits can be seen in the following example:

> The manager of a ski resort hotel whose market is primarily skiers must be concerned about the seasonal nature of the business. Off season the facilities are idle. To deal with this problem the resort might build golf and tennis facilities to attract summer resort guests. By so doing it creates a combinatorial benefit between the winter ski market and the resort market, providing for stable profits throughout the year. Even if neither group by itself can generate enough revenue, the two groups together can be profitable. The firm's physical resource, its hotel, is effectively used.
>
> This portfolio effect has two important characteristics. First, both markets use the same resource. Each market fills a void left by the other, putting excess resources to work. But there may be no further interaction between the two markets; if ski traffic increases, it will not affect summer resort occupancy.
>
> But the combinatorial benefit of the two sets of hotel visitors may not be limited to the complement effect. If skiers find that the hotel is a good place to stay, some may return in the summer. And summer guests may decide to try the ski resort next winter. One market is able to ride free on the invisible asset (the hotel's reputation) developed by the other. Sales in one market (skiers) are no longer independent of those in the other (summer guests). The effect may be positive or negative, but it is very different from the complement effect.... It is multiplicative rather than additive; this is synergy.
>
> (p. 42)

2.2.3 Synergy and superior corporate performance

An important distinction between physical and invisible assets, and between complementary and synergy benefits, lies in the difficulty competitors have in imitating invisible assets. Using underutilised plant to produce another product will provide a reasonably certain payoff, but these benefits are ultimately limited by the plant's capacity. Using cash cows to fund stars may provide a secure source of finance, but the strategy can be copied by competitors. Complementary benefits are unlikely to be lasting sources of superior performance for a corporation: competitors are likely to achieve similar complementary benefits. Invisible, information-based assets, on the other hand, are capable of being used repeatedly, and in innovative combinations, as a powerful long-term source of superior corporate performance, because they are more likely to remain unique to the corporation.

This is demonstrated by the history of Hoechst's pharmaceutical division. Founded on strong skills in organic chemistry research in the nineteenth century, Hoescht's research laboratories were completely destroyed by bombs between 1943 and 1945. Despite the destruction of these physical assets, and the lack of financial capital in the immediate post-war years, Hoescht quickly reassembled its research capabilities – the true source of its pharmaceutical success. This enabled Hoescht to re-emerge as a leader in organic chemistry-based pharmaceuticals, with successful products such as Lasix and Orinase (Bogner and Thomas, 1994).

2.2.4 Synergy across time

Synergy and complementary combination benefits must be dynamic to persist. Static combination benefits in corporate strategy exist from integrating two different strategies at one point in time. Dynamic combination benefits, on the other hand, result from integrating two different strategies across time (see Figure 2.1).

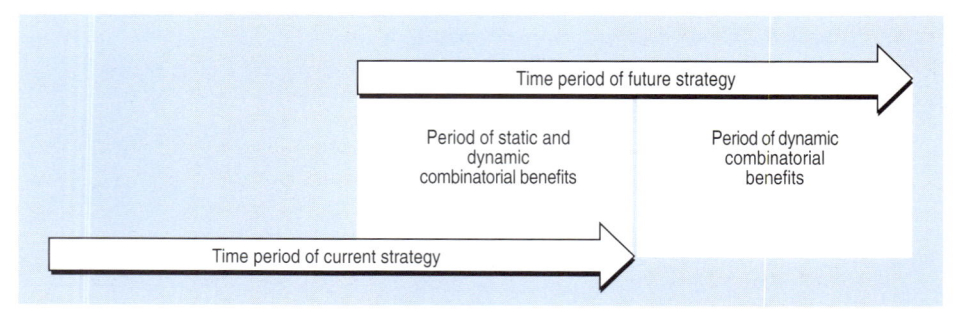

Figure 2.1 Dynamic and static combinations of strategies

Effective dynamic strategy builds resources, both physical and invisible assets, to enable future strategic resource requirements to be met. The stock of resources and capabilities an organisation can call on is, however, path- and time-dependent. Any choice of strategy requires investment in research, technologies, equipment, human skills or knowledge. It changes the set of resources and capabilities available thereafter and has an opportunity cost – the value of the strategic options no longer available. In Itami's words, 'the future stock of resources is the variable that connects present and future strategies. ... If the current and future strategies mesh well they create a dynamic complement effect or a dynamic synergy effect, or both' (p. 48). (See Figure 2.2.)

Just as static complement benefits are obtained from combining physical assets to ensure full utilisation, so with *dynamic complement benefits*, for example:

- Gravel and aggregates extraction pits have prospered during the years of intensive road-building in Western Europe. The same exhausted pits have found a new, profitable use as waste management depositories, creating a dynamic complement combination benefit.

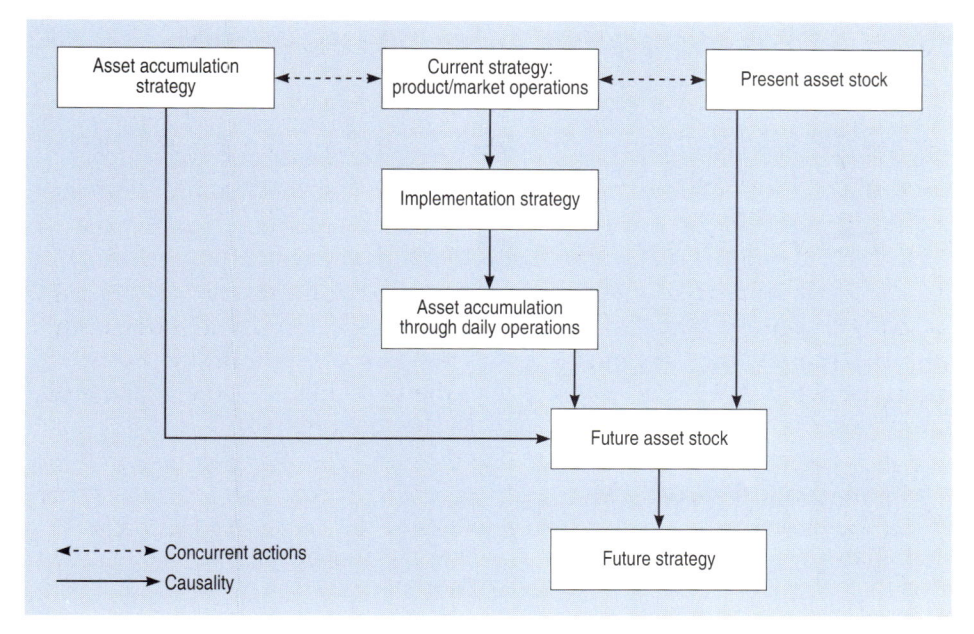

Figure 2.2 A basic framework for dynamic combinatorial benefits

- The Trans Alaskan Pipeline was built to serve North Alaska's 'elephant' oil field, Prudhoe Bay. As production from this oil field declined, dynamic complement benefits were obtained by using spare pipeline capacity to transport oil from smaller, more marginal fields such as Kuparuk and Niakuk.

Dynamic synergy benefits, based on re-usable invisible assets, are more likely to be a sustainable source of superior corporate performance:

- When Coca-Cola entered the Japanese market after 1945, it offered a bottling franchise to Kirin Beer. This was in line with Coke's strategy of not owning facilities, choosing firms with bottling capacity and strong finances as franchisees to fund its world-wide expansion. The aim was to gain rapid access to existing physical assets. Kirin Beer, on the other hand, was looking for a way to enter the non-alcoholic drink markets, of which it had no experience. Through its Coke franchise, it gained knowledge of both marketing techniques and production processes. This knowledge and technical expertise were used dynamically when Kirin anticipated changes in Japanese tastes in favour of fruit juice drinks in advance of Coca-Cola. Coca-Cola lost Japanese market share to Kirin.

- Until 1977, Ricoh was best known as a photocopier manufacturer. Its optical imaging skills derived from its original capabilities in camera manufacture. It had, however, neglected the less attractive camera market, and its Japanese market share had declined from 65 per cent in 1955 to 3 per cent in 1977. At this time Ricoh decided it wanted to diversify into other consumer electronics products. It then deliberately refocused on its camera business, building market share and a brand reputation for quality consumer electronics products which then allowed it to successfully diversify into other consumer products.

Itami believes that the interaction between invisible assets and dynamic synergy is a virtuous circle:

> To create dynamic synergy, a firm should choose activities that create invisible assets, design strategy with dynamic synergy in mind, and go beyond its current abilities to develop these invisible assets.
>
> *(Itami, 1992 p. 52)*

2.3 STRATEGIC CAPABILITIES AND CORPORATE STRATEGY

The remark that ended the last section, that a corporation should 'go beyond its current abilities' to develop invisible assets should remind you of Hamel and Prahalad's Course Reader article for Book 1, 'Strategy as stretch and leverage'. Itami echoes this concept of 'stretch' in his discussion of static and dynamic physical and invisible assets. The previous section should also have reminded you of our discussion on resources, capabilities, distinctive competencies, competitive advantage and sustainability in Books 4 and 5. Prahalad and Hamel have explored the role that competencies play in corporate strategy.

You should now read their article, 'The core competence of the corporation', in the Course Reader.

2.3.1 What are core competencies?

Prahalad and Hamel view the corporation as a collection of core competencies and core products, rather than as a portfolio of businesses defined by product–market boundaries. Their hierarchy of end products, businesses, core products and core competencies sees competencies as the 'roots of competitiveness' for the corporation across time:

> Core competence does not diminish with use. Unlike physical assets, which do deteriorate over time, competencies are enhanced as they are applied and shared.
>
> *(Prahalad and Hamel, Course Reader)*

The importance of enhancing core competencies through use means corporate competition should be defined in terms of core- rather than end-product markets. Re-using core products and enhancing core competencies across a combination of businesses and end products also provides an alternative rationale for corporate diversification: instead of entering markets because of their attractiveness, corporations should enter new markets to exploit and develop a core competence which is a source of superior performance. Indeed, Hamel and Prahalad see competition to develop core competencies (and new core products) as a corporate battle for the future. They call this 'competing for industry foresight' (Hamel and Prahalad, 1994).

Core competencies are thus a feature of corporate, rather than business, strategy. The concept is, however, rooted in the same field as the discussion of competing with resources and capabilities that you encountered in Book 4. Consider the tests of core competence:

1. Core competencies provide potential access to a wide variety of markets.
2. Core competencies make a significant contribution to the perceived customer benefits of the end product.
3. Core competencies should be difficult for competitors to imitate.

The second test establishes that a competence is competitively significant, while the third implies it should be a source of sustainable competitive advantage; these could easily apply to capabilities at a business strategy level. It is the first test, which implies that a core competence is transferable, that highlights it as a source of *corporate* superior performance: it is a source of combination benefits. Further, when we take tests 1 and 3 together, we establish that a core competence is likely to be a source of dynamic synergy.

Activity 2.4

You should be familiar with the commonplace injunction that businesses should be market, rather than product orientated. Prahalad and Hamel talk of core products as the embodiment of competencies, and end products as mere applications of these competencies. Indeed, corporations competing with core competencies often seem to serve a disparate mixture of end-product markets. These corporations seem to ignore the opposition between market and (end) product orientation. From what you have read, do you think this is justified?

Discussion

Prahalad and Hamel's advice is significantly different from calls for corporations to redefine their businesses in terms of 'marketing needs served'. The most influential of these calls was that of Theodore Levitt (1960), who believed that too many companies concentrated on selling the products they had, rather than on meeting the needs of the customers they served. This delineated the opposition between product and market orientations. Levitt considered that businesses became obsolete as new technologies, skills and changes in customer needs made their products obsolete. Businesses needed to define themselves in terms of customer needs served and adapt their technologies and products accordingly.

The US rail corporations after 1945, for example, continued to define their business in terms of their product (rail travel), rather than in terms of customer needs (transportation and communication). As the railways declined, Levitt argued they should have moved into 'cars, trucks, airplanes, even telephones'. This ignores the difficulty in acquiring the appropriate technologies and skills – far less the distinctive competencies which could be a source of advantage – of such businesses. Flying an airline, running a trucking fleet and operating a telephone network require different resources and capabilities from those the railways possessed. Better to enhance core competencies and search for new end-product applications for these.

> For example, while SKF, the world's leading manufacturer of roller bearings, might be tempted to define its core competence as bearings, such a definition would be unnecessarily limiting in terms of access to new markets. No doubt, SKF engineers and marketers have considered all the potential uses of roller bearings. Fortunately, the company's growth is not totally dependent on finding new uses for roller bearings, because when SKF moves away from a product-based view of its competencies, to a skill-based view, new opportunities quickly emerge. SKF has competencies in anti-friction (understanding how different materials work together to either generate or reduce friction); in precision engineering (it is one of the very few European companies that can machine hard metals to incredibly tight tolerances); and in making perfectly spherical devices ... the point is simple: to increase its potential 'opportunity horizon' a firm must be able to move beyond an orthodox, product-centric view of its competencies.
>
> (Hamel, 1994, pp. 15–16)

The competitive drift that may occur from defining a business in terms of end products or markets, may also occur in attempts to redefine the 'core businesses' of corporations without analysing core competencies carefully. For example, the desire to diversify drove many oil and gas corporations to redefine their business as 'extraction'; they then acquired minerals and coal businesses. The competencies necessary to find, produce and process minerals and coal are not the same as those in oil and gas, however. This may not have seemed a problem since oil and gas production and processing skills are also distinct. Oil and gas are, however, invariably found in combination, and oil and gas corporations accumulated these disparate competencies over seventy years. The acquisitions of coal and minerals businesses were not a success, and were eventually divested.

Activity 2.5

Review the Volkswagen Group mini-case that opened Section 2 of this book. From the information in the mini-case, construct a diagram which shows the hierarchy of competencies, core products, businesses, and end products that constitute the VW group. Refer to the Prahalad and Hamel Course Reader article on core competencies which you have just read for the structure of the hierarchy diagram. Once you have done this, read the following addendum to the mini-case, and analyse the potential problems which you can identify in VW's corporate strategy of seeking to standardise parts and assemblies across the group, using Prahalad and Hamel's framework.

MINI-CASE ADDENDUM: FOUR WHEELS AT VOLKSWAGEN?

VW's corporate strategy had raised a number of queries amongst commentators about the problems and dangers it would face:

- The productivity gains from introducing new models were potentially worthless if surplus labour still had to be employed. The political restraints on VW's use of its German labour force meant that the benefits from introducing the new VW Polo, for example, could not be fully realised. The new Polo could be assembled in 16 hours, as opposed to 25 hours for the old model. What was VW to do, however, with its underemployed labour?

- There were a number of marketing dangers in the standardisation strategy. Firstly, if the Audi brand cars were increasingly seen as of the same lineage as the mid-market VW brand, this could damage Audi's sporty, high-tech image. Secondly, the upgrading of SEAT's and Skoda's images might mean that their VW-designed compact and sub-compact cars would increasingly compete against and undercut VW's own Polo and Golf models. This created a danger of VW cannibalising its markets if the distinctiveness of the separate brand identities was compromised by the standardisation programme.

- Audi had designed the A3 and A4 models to be extremely rigid at high speeds on German autobahns. For the less expensive SEAT and Skoda models aimed at the family marketplace, such rigid floorpans were arguably inappropriate and unnecessarily expensive.

- In their review of the new VW Passat in November 1996, the BBC's influential 'Top Gear' programme noted the excellence of the car (based on the Audi A4) and suggested that family car market leaders such as the Ford Mondeo and Opel Vectra would be under threat. More significantly, the reviewer also suggested that the Passat was good enough to compete in the executive car segment and threaten the class-leading A4.

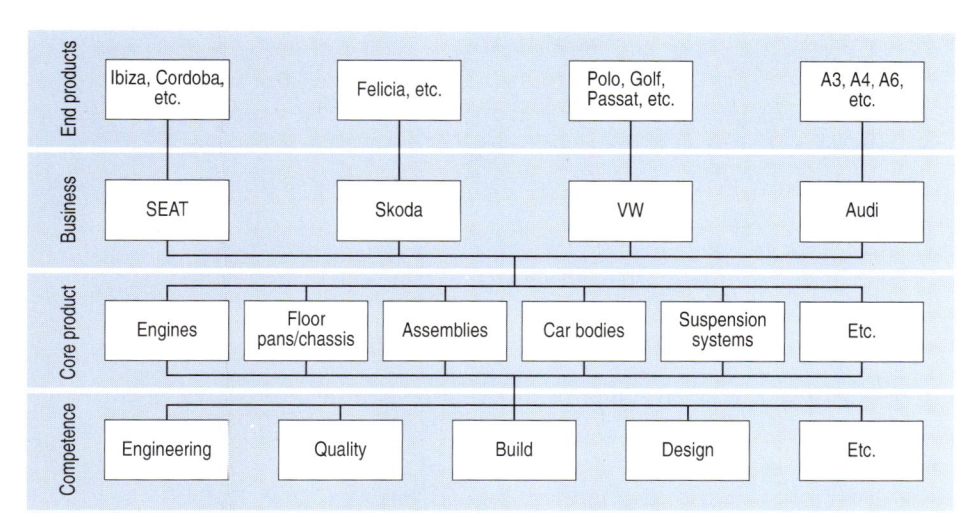

Figure 2.3 VW Group mini-case: competencies, core products, businesses, end products

Discussion

The diagram we have constructed can be seen as Figure 2.3. This is based on the information in the mini-case.

Information about the utilisation of VW's core competencies across the group is limited in the case, but there is evidence that VW's design, quality, engineering and building skills have been influential in upgrading the reputations of SEAT and Skoda. There is also some evidence that the skills that Audi has used to reinvigorate its end products may well be transferable to the new VW Golf and Passat models to be based on them.

The mini-case is much clearer, however, that the VW group strategy is based on the standardisation of a number of important sub-assemblies, which equate with 'core products' in Prahalad and Hamel's scheme. While the mini-case does not use the language of Prahalad and Hamel, it is reasonable to assume that standardisation of core products should lead to the enhancement of the VW group's core competencies, as 'core products are the embodiment of core competencies'. It is unclear, however, to what degree VW's competencies are distinctive or difficult for competitors to imitate.

It is when we consider the test that core competence should provide access to a wide variety of markets, that we see potential problems in VW's standardisation strategy. The standardisation of core products across the different market segments served by the VW group may simply blur the boundaries between their end-product markets. VW has already experienced this problem to some extent, with competition between the acclaimed VW Polo, SEAT Ibiza and Skoda Felicia models, and it looked likely to arise with the VW Passat and Audi A4. The problem was not unique to VW: when the PSA Group's Citroën Saxo and Peugeot 106 sub-compacts were released in 1996 reviewers saw them as variants of the same car.

This evolving problem of the increasing similarity of end products indicates the importance of leveraging core competencies and core products across *distinct end products to realise the full potential of core competencies. Compare VW with the example of Honda used by Prahalad and Hamel. Honda are considered to have key core competencies in the design and manufacture of combustion engines and powertrains. This has led them into a number of seemingly unrelated businesses – motorcycles, outboard motors for boats, portable generators and lawnmowers – where the end-product leverage of their core competencies and products is never in doubt. In these distinct end-product markets, separate brands are not needed for distinctiveness. Indeed, Honda gains from its reputation by using the Honda brand across all end products.*

2.3.2 Core competence competition

Studies of diversification have, until recently, tended to discuss corporate strategy in terms of end products and markets rather than core competencies. Rumelt (1974) measured the performance of seven types of diversified US corporation in the period 1949 to 1969. Rumelt's results show the highest correlation (but not a causal relationship) between superior performance and 'related constrained' diversifications, which are those where businesses 'draw on the same common core skill, strength, or resource'.

Rumelt is one of the chief proponents of the view that distinctive resources and capabilities are an important source of superior performance (remember the Rumelt Course Reader article for Book 3). Reviewing Prahalad and Hamel's work, he established four key components of core competence competition (Rumelt, 1994, p. xv):

1. *Corporate span* – Core competencies span businesses and products within a corporation.
2. *Temporal dominance* – Products are only the momentary expression of core competencies. Competencies are more stable and evolve more slowly than products.
3. *Learning-by-doing* – Competencies are gained and enhanced by use.
4. *Competitive locus* – Product–market competition is merely the superficial expression of a deeper competition over competencies.

The power of the core competence approach is that it provides a coherent view of how superior corporate performance can be achieved, allows for the importance of the strategic actions of managers, and captures the *dynamic* nature of strategy.

3 DIVERSIFICATION AND DIVESTMENT

Corporate strategy is fundamentally concerned with achieving superior performance from *combining* business activities. As a consequence, corporate strategy also often involves decisions to seek better combinations: to diversify activities, or to divest existing activities that no longer promote superior corporate performance.

3.1 DIVERSIFICATION STRATEGIES

You should now read Chapter 15 of the Set Book, which takes a close look at corporate diversification strategies.

Activity 3.1

Review the Set Book chapter on diversification strategies. Summarise Grant's argument as to the main motives for corporate diversification, the nature of the benefits from diversification, and the tests that should be applied to determine whether a corporation should diversify or not. Create a diagram which maps your summary.

Discussion

Grant states that the two routes to superior performance that we identified earlier in the course – entering an attractive industry and possessing a competitive advantage – apply to corporate strategy as they do to business strategy. Grant then examines the possible motives for diversification:

1. growth – *which he discounts as primarily a managerial objective (as we discussed in Book 2)*
2. investment risk-spreading – *which he identifies as being in the interests of managers and lenders, but not of owners (except in the special circumstances where internal financing is cheaper)*
3. profitability – *which he says should be evaluated against Porter's (1987) three tests for diversification value-creation.*

Porter's 'attractiveness' and 'cost-of-entry' tests are likely to mean that value-creation cannot easily occur in a competitive market for corporate control. If a possible diversification does meet the attractiveness and cost-of-entry tests alone, then an opportunistic cheap acquisition may be appropriate.

It is Porter's 'better-off' test, however, which provides the best rationale for diversification, and this depends on establishing that there is advantage available from combining the separate businesses. The sources of benefits are then examined, and while the importance of market power is acknowledged, it is economies of scope that Grant focuses on as the main source of corporate superior performance. Economies of scope will occur by combining businesses – either through the ability to better utilise the physical capacity of tangible resources between activities, or through the transfer of re-usable intangible resources, or organisational capabilities.

Such economies of scope are not enough, however, to justify a diversification decision alone, and Grant adds a further test – the economies of scope must be more cheaply obtained through internalising the business activities (using the transaction cost economics theory we encountered in Book 4).

Refer back to the Glaxo mini-case in Book 1. Glaxo used Hoffman La Roche's sales force to launch their 'blockbuster' drug, Zantac, in the United States. Glaxo had no US sales force; Hoffman La Roche were faced with the patent expiry of all their major drugs. Scope economies were available from combining the underutilised Hoffman La Roche sales force and Glaxo's unique marketing approach. Glaxo could have developed their own sales force, but the transaction costs of doing so – notably the time delay – were prohibitive compared with sourcing the sales force outside the company.

The benefits from internalising transactions within a corporation include efficiencies in creating a corporate market in labour and capital resources and from gaining proprietary access to important information and knowledge.

This argument is summarised in Figure 3.1.

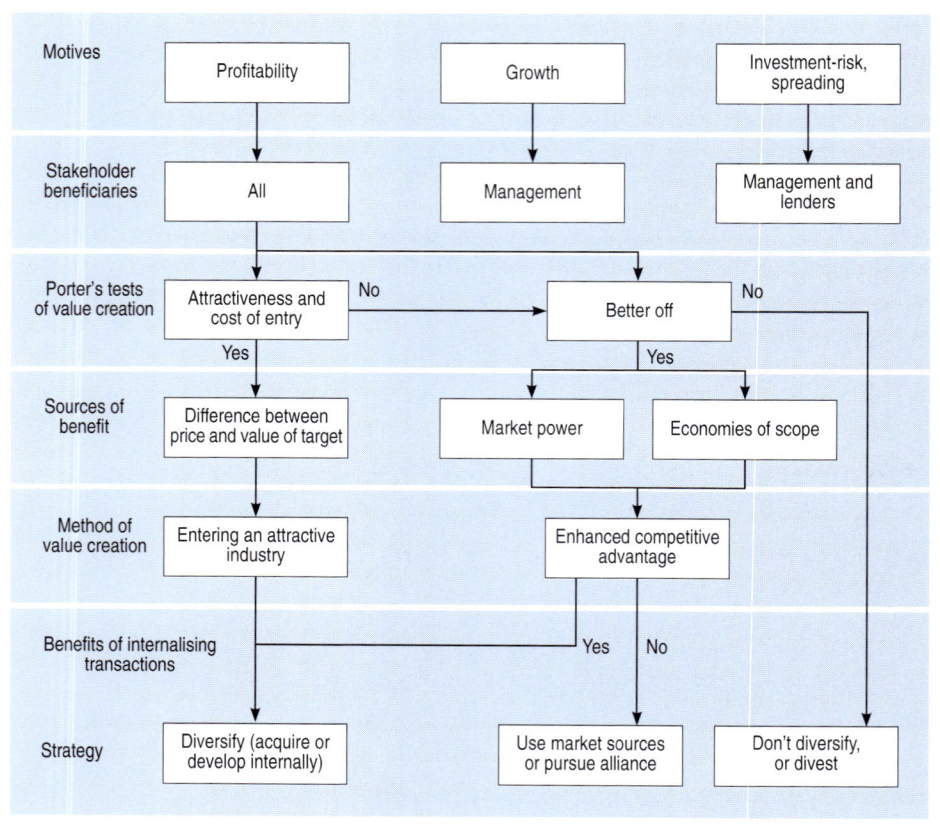

Figure 3.1   Motives, benefits and the tests of diversification strategies

Grant's double test for diversification to obtain enhanced competitive advantage (the availability of both economies of scope from combining the complementary activities, and transaction economies from internalising the combination) is a very effective tool for choosing an appropriate corporate strategy. The introduction of the 'make or buy' test of transaction cost economics highlights the fact that economies of scope may be available from combining separate activities in ways other than by owning them (recall, for example, Benetton's approach to managing its Value Chain, discussed in Book 4). We will return to the role of networks and alliances later in this book. For now, however, note the emphasis Grant places on the importance of economies of scope in providing benefits from combining discrete business activities.

3.2 DIVESTMENT

The sale or disposal of one of a corporation's activities is known as *divestment*. Divestments may occur when corporate synergies no longer exist, underutilised corporate assets can be better deployed elsewhere, or core competencies cannot be enhanced by leverage across the corporation. Many divestments occur when subsidiary businesses show decline, and the next sub-section will consider whether divestment is, indeed, the correct response to failing businesses.

3.2.1 Decline: divestment or recovery?

Portfolio theory suggests that businesses that make a positive cash contribution ('cash cows'), and those that, with investment, should mature into such businesses ('stars'), have secure positions in a portfolio based on cash flow synergies. 'Dogs' are deemed to be making only diminishing returns to cash flow. The theory recommends divestment of these businesses. The simple solution of divesting portfolio 'dogs' has come in for criticism, however, by those who believe such businesses can hold considerable value.

Kathy Harrigan (1988) sees declining industries as opportunities for *end-game strategies*. Depending on how attractive an industry in decline is (see Table 3.1), and on whether the business has competitive strengths in remaining attractive market niches or segments, four possible end-game strategies are recommended (see Figure 3.2).

Table 3.1 The attractiveness of declining industries

Favourable conditions	Unfavourable conditions
• Demand-price insensitive	• Demand-price sensitive
• Long-term market for replacement products	• Demand could deteriorate abruptly
• Customer loyalty likely to persist	• Low customer switching costs
• Revitalisation likely, albeit remote	• Competition volatile
• Firm serves protected market niches	• Competitors face high exit barriers
• Suppliers willing to help firm compete	• Customers have high bargaining power

	Competitive strengths in attractive niches	No competitive strengths in attractive niches
Favourable industry structure and demand conditions	Leadership	Harvest or niche
Unfavourable industry structure and demand conditions	Harvest or niche	Quick sale

Figure 3.2   End-game strategies

The end-game strategies are:

1. *Leadership* – A leadership strategy is dependent on achieving market power within the remaining attractive segments of the industry, and controlling the process of decline in the business's favour. This strategy requires some investment. The expectation is that, as other competitors leave the industry, so the profitability of the remaining firms improves.

2. *Niche* – Niche strategies depend on the existence of defensible market segments. In an end-game, the strategy requires a business to pull out of the broad market and concentrate on niches where it has relative competitive strengths, or where customer demand is likely to persist longer (or at higher levels) than in the rest of the industry.

3. *Quick sale* – Corporations should seek a quick sale when it is likely to realise the greatest value from a weak competitive position in an unfavourable environment. In these instances, delay in selling may destroy remaining value.

4. *Harvest* – Harvesting assumes that value can be returned to a corporation from a business by continuing to run it to extract as much cash as possible. Further investment is not expected: the objective is to realise the maximum cash from the business.

3.2.2   Turnarounds

Harrigan believes corporations must 'flee or fight' in declining industries. Leadership and niche strategies are the choice of those who fight. For those who flee, the choice is between quick sale or harvesting in the timing and method of divestment. Her work, however, accepts the industry life-cycle assumption of a predetermined path to extinction.

However, studies (such as Slatter, 1984) of businesses (as opposed to Harrigan's industries) in decline have shown that successful recovery or turnaround is possible; divesting a struggling subsidiary is not pre-ordained. Grinyer *et al.* (1988) studied the strategies followed by companies where 'a period of stagnation or decline *relative to competitors* in their industries was ... followed by a dramatic and sustained improvement which resulted in their outperforming their rivals'. They called these companies 'sharpbenders' (defined as companies that achieve a sharp and sustained improvement in performance) and the strategies they most commonly reported included:

- major changes in management
- stronger financial controls
- new product–market focus
- improved marketing
- significant reductions in production costs
- improved quality and service.

These are remarkably similar to the key turnaround strategies recommended by Slatter (1984) and discussed in Book 9.

Although the sharpbenders also reported efforts to diversify, make acquisitions, and reduce debt, these strategies were not adopted as frequently as in control companies within the same industries. Grinyer *et al.* noted that sharpbenders stood out *significantly* from control companies in three respects:

1 More improved their marketing.
2 More reduced their production costs.
3 Fewer pursued acquisition as a route to change.

While many of the control companies studied took many of the same actions, sharpbenders succeeded 'because of the range and effectiveness of the measures they used and the *timing* of them'. To illustrate sharpbending strategies, read the following mini-case taken from their study. It describes the strategies followed by MacAllan-Glenlivet, a family-owned, single-product company which had no alternative but to improve its business. It is interesting to speculate whether a larger corporation would have divested this business, if it were a small, unrelated subsidiary.

MINI-CASE: MACALLAN-GLENLIVET PLC

This small company operates as a 'family firm' with a single product – a malt whisky known as The MacAllan.

1 History of the firm

Throughout the 1970s, world trade in Scotch whisky maintained a strong upward trend, reaching an exceptional peak in 1978. From 1978 to 1983, in an environment of widespread recession, sales declined. Since 1978 it has been the proprietary blends – bottled in Scotland – that have borne the brunt of decreasing sales.

Malts, on the other hand, although they represent a small proportion of Scotch whisky sales, have shown a sustained growth through the 1970s as their high quality has become more widely appreciated by consumers. Hence, distillers who were able to make the switch in the 1970s from output based on blend to output of single malts were able to switch into a growing market.

As MacAllan is small (46 employees) it has always been closely run. It had grown steadily since the Second World War. While some of their whisky had always been set aside for bottled sales, in 1968 the board decided to lay down larger stocks since whisky has to mature for ten years before it can be sold in bottled form. For blending it is sold as soon as it is distilled and put in the barrel. Although, MacAllan made this switch in 1968 it still faced a crisis in 1974/5 when demand for blending fell throughout the industry.

II Causes of the relative decline

The causes of MacAllan's decline are simple:

1. depressed demand in the sector; and
2. loss of a major customer taking 30 per cent of output.

III Triggers for sharpbending

Depressed industry demand affected MacAllan with the loss of a major customer; also many other blenders reduced the level of their future order for source whisky for blending.

IV Actions taken to promote sharpbending

(a) *Change of accountant/tighter financial controls.* The crisis occurred within a few months of the appointment of Willie Phillips (later to become Managing Director) as Management Accountant. While financial control methods were already in place, he introduced much tighter controls on day-to-day cash flows.

(b) *Marketing switch.* The dangers of concentrating on blenders for the bulk of their output led to a switch to the production of single malt in bottle form. The marketing switch was simple to implement, since the firm had plenty of raw-material stocks.

(c) *Rationalisation of the labour force.* There were a few redundancies in the workforce, which proved difficult to make in a tight, family-controlled firm.

(d) *Investments.* During the crisis the firm continued to invest in both energy-saving and labour-saving equipment. These investments were funded mainly by bank loans.

V Continuing characteristics of sharpbending

(a) *Marketing philosophy.* The marketing switch made during the crisis in the recession was the cornerstone of recovery. A Marketing Director appointed in 1978 was able to initiate a staggering 30 per cent per annum growth rate for five years. Sequential attacks were made on the most promising markets via agency agreements. Such agreements allowed them to continue as a small company unhindered by administrative overheads.

The product is promoted at the quality end of the market, based on the water and the method of distilling rather than creative marketing.

(b) *Financial planning model.* The company operates detailed financial models coupled to ten-year forecasts, which the ten-year lag from production to sale necessitates. The model incorporates a very tight annual cash-flow plan, involving monthly reporting. The emphasis is on the control of cash rather than on the profit/loss account.

(c) *Further energy-saving investments.* The company has continued its cost-cutting programme of energy-saving investments.

VI Conclusion

MacAllan suffered the fate of an intermediate market supplier during depression of demand for the final product. Rationalisation, reorganisation and cost-cutting strategies brought such strong recovery that during the further 1979/80 industry recession, the company experienced minimum disruption, while other local distillers closed.

(Adapted from Grinyer et al., 1988, pp. 232–4)

3.2.3 Divestment and core competencies

As portfolio theory has become less influential, rationales for divestment decisions have changed. In Section 2 we showed corporations increasingly identifying businesses which they see as core. The concept of core competencies can, therefore, provide a useful rationale to determine which activities should be retained within a corporation. If a competence is core to a corporation, it is a strategic focus for long-term competition for market share of core products. A corporation should not normally seek to divest activities which enhance its core competencies.

If, however, an activity or business does not involve a core competence, a corporation should seriously consider whether it should divest the activity. It is here that 'make or buy' tests of transaction costs can be used to test divestments: can the activity be more efficiently carried out within the corporation, or by outside partners or contractors? The test of efficiency is not measured in purely financial terms, but should include all potential managerial efficiencies.

'Outsourcing' is a divestment strategy which recognises that improved effectiveness might come from buying in non-core competencies. Such improved effectiveness rests on the better skills, resources and expertise of partners or contractors for whom particular activities do constitute core competencies, or on the opening up of a non-core activity to market-based competition, rather than continuing an internal monopoly. Outsourcing has provided opportunities for both divestors and suppliers of services:

- British Telecom and the US telecoms corporation MCI (now part of WorldCom) formed an alliance to promote an international service specialising in the management of Wide Area Networks for major multinational corporations.
- Many corporations have turned to outsourcing specialists to run their information systems. Among these, BP has employed Arthur Andersen and the UK's tax collection agency's system is operated by EDS.

The outsourcing of information systems raises serious questions for corporations over what constitutes a strategic asset, the competitive security of information and knowledge, and what are or are not core competencies. (You may wish to return to Book 4 at this point to refresh your understanding of the issues affecting strategic assets, and the disadvantages as well as the advantages of outsourcing.)

3.2.4 Divestment in the public sector

The issue of what constitutes a proper activity to be outsourced also underpins much of the controversy surrounding the privatisation and deregulation of public services, a form of divestment by the state. Public sector divestment initiatives have come in many forms. Examples include:

- UK financial services regulators, such as FIMBRA, operate as self-regulating industry bodies, unlike the US Securities and Exchange Commission, which is a government department.
- The US prison service has been opened up to private companies, who operate penal establishments on behalf of the government.

Divestment of state activities is often controversial and heavily influenced by political ideologies, which differ in the extent to which they think the state should be involved in economic and social activity at all. This makes it difficult for managers to apply clinically the rational tests of diversification we have discussed above.

4 Strategies for corporate structure

In Book 8 we discussed Alfred Chandler's (1962) thesis that 'structure follows strategy'. Our interest here is with Chandler's historical analysis of the innovations of four US corporations – General Motors, DuPont, Sears and Exxon – in developing divisionalised corporate structures in the 1920s and 1930s to deal with the problems of size and complexity arising from their strategies of rapid growth and diversification. The structures developed by managers such as Alfred Sloan at General Motors (Sloan, 1963) were amongst the most significant competitive innovations of the twentieth century. They showed how to follow complex diversification strategies while providing a simple, clear structure to manage the corporation.

Rumelt (1974) commented that, for some, structure does follow strategy; for others, 'structure follows fashion'. The gradual diffusion of the divisionalised structure meant that it remained a source of superior performance until the 1970s, by which time it had been adopted by most diversified corporations (Armour and Teece, 1986).

The divisionalised structure was significant as the first recorded strategic management tool designed specifically for the task of the corporate manager. In some senses, corporate strategy as a management activity originated with this innovation. It is to the tools for managing corporate strategy that we now turn.

4.1 THE STRUCTURES OF CORPORATIONS

You should now read 'The structure of the multibusiness company' in the Set Book, on pages 389–392.

The Set Book gives a good account of the arguments in favour of the divisionalised corporate structure. Grant suggests, however, that reconciling simultaneous co-ordination and decentralisation is, in practice, less than easy. We can conjecture, therefore, that the form may be most successful when the need for corporate co-ordination, of the type implied by a core competencies approach, is minimised. The main strength of the divisionalised corporation seems to be the clarity and simplicity of its structure, which treats the corporation as an unconnected series of businesses. Whilst ideal for a corporation using portfolio strategies where the only synergies sought are financial, it may be inadequate where corporate benefits are sought from leveraging invisible assets or core competencies. We shall return to this problem later in this book.

4.2 ALTERNATIVE INFLUENCES ON CORPORATE STRATEGY AND STRUCTURE

The divisionalised corporation has been primarily studied in the Anglo-American ('Anglo') economies. Such studies may be highly context-specific. What happens where the context is different? For example:

- What might be the impact on the strategy and structure of a corporation of operating within a country where the regulatory environment differs from the 'Anglo' model? What complexities arise when a corporation operates in a number of different regulatory environments?

- The 'Anglo' economies enjoyed relatively long periods of economic prosperity and growth, and of social and political stability during much of the twentieth century. This pattern was unusual in comparison with many other economies. Might the divisionalised structures have evolved differently if the strategic issues facing corporations were different?

- The 'Anglo' corporation is embedded in a model of capitalism that many argue is culturally specific. What other types of corporation have evolved where the norms of capitalism are different?

The sub-sections that follow will explore some of the alternative contexts where strategies of corporate diversification have not automatically produced divisionalisation.

4.2.1 Regulation and corporate strategy

The institutional influence of government regulation affects decisions about corporate strategy and structure, particularly where activities span borders and are influenced by the laws and regulations of a number of countries. Regulation, regulatory changes and government action also create opportunities for organisations to exploit. For example, the opening of government supply contracts to all organisations in the European Union means that private Italian construction companies build motorways for public-sector agencies in Scotland. However, regulation and policy also create constraints and difficulties, since bidding for government supply contracts requires bidders to meet standards for quality, performance and disclosure that may differ from those of the private sector.

An example of a venture where cross-border government regulations and actions have created both corporate strategy opportunities and constraints is given in the following mini-case of Grupo Domos and Etecsa. Grupo Domos and Etecsa operate in a volatile environment. Considerable political uncertainty surrounds the relationship between the USA and Cuba, as Cuban exiles represent a significant ethnic grouping in any US election.

> ### MINI-CASE: GRUPO DOMOS AND ETECSA
>
> The US trade embargo on Cuba had been in force for over thirty years by the mid-1990s. The Cuban economy, which had prospered reasonably as a siege economy in the years of favourable trade terms with the Soviet Union, faced a precipitous collapse after massive Soviet subsidies were withdrawn after 1990. Cuba's President Fidel Castro turned to foreign investment as a means of stimulating economic activity in Cuba, and started privatising state-owned assets. The US trade embargo, imposed in retaliation for the nationalisation

of US-owned Cuban assets after the 1959 Cuban revolution, forbade any US-owned or resident company or individual from trading with, or investing in, Cuba. This forced Cuba to turn to nations which had retained ties with the island, such as Canada, Mexico, Venezuela, and Spain, for new investment funds. One such deal was the $750 million acquisition in 1994 by Mexico's privately owned Grupo Domos conglomerate of a 49 per cent stake in, and management control of, Cuba's dilapidated national telephone monopoly Etecsa. This stake was held through a Grupo Domos subsidiary, Citel. The deal called on Grupo Domos to fund the upgrading of Cuba's domestic network, from an average of three to ten phones per 100 Cubans by 2001.

The Cuban Democracy Act, passed by the US Congress in 1992, called for a tightening of anti-Cuban sanctions, but simultaneously sought to promote 'people-to-people' contacts between the US and Cuba, aimed at opening up Cuba's relatively closed society to the ideals of US democracy and capitalism. This meant the end of unilateral US rationing of bilateral telephone contact with Cuba. The Act also allowed US long-distance telecoms companies such as AT&T, MCI, Sprint, and WorldCom to install many more modern direct dial lines to Cuba.

This unwittingly created a hard currency bonanza for Etecsa and Grupo Domos as international telecoms treaties call for the equal division of bilateral traffic revenues, regardless of the point of origin of the traffic: in the US–Cuban situation over 99 per cent of calls originated in the US, and were paid for in US dollars. The growth in call volume to Cuba was far in excess of all predictions, rising from 400 calls per day prior to deregulation in 1994, to 50,000 calls daily in 1995. Etecsa's profits for 1995, budgeted at $34 million, rose to $120 million in practice. Further, while these revenues were earned in hard currency, Etecsa's employees were paid in devaluing Cuban pesos.

For Grupo Domos, however, the celebration was quickly over. The US government's trade embargo and the 1992 legislation had created a marvellous arbitrage opportunity in its corporate holding of Etecsa, but the Mexican government's handling of its debt scheduling problems and the subsequent devaluation of the Mexican peso in November 1994 changed its corporate strategy in relation to Etecsa. The collapse of the Mexican peso made it extremely difficult for Grupo Domos to use its peso-denominated cash flows – now much reduced in exchange value terms – from its Mexican tourism and waste management activities to finance its US dollar denominated commitments to invest in Etecsa. In January 1996, Grupo Domos was ten months overdue on $300 million of its purchase payment for Etecsa, and on a $196 million commitment to fund the upgrading of Cuba's domestic telephone system.

Cuba's government was a patient creditor in this period, insisting that the venture, and the policy of selling privatised stakes to foreign investors, was successful. Grupo Domos were, however, forced into selling some of their interest in Etecsa to fund its dollar commitments to Cuba. The forced corporate restructuring programme included:

1. The sale of a 25 per cent stake in Citel (which holds its 49 per cent stake in Etecsa) to the Italian national telephone company STET for $281 million.
2. The proposed sale of a further 24 per cent stake in Citel. This would still leave Grupo Domos with a 51 per cent controlling stake in Citel and, thus, in its Cuban venture.
3. The 'last resort' step of selling minority holdings in Grupo Domos itself.

(Adapted from International Business Week, 29 January 1996)

The essence of Grupo Domos' strategy was to exploit a financial cross-border arbitrage opportunity. It used apparently relatively stable Mexican peso revenues as security for hard currency US dollars to acquire its Cuban investment. Operating expenditures were then financed in the collapsing Cuban peso, to access a US dollar revenue stream, heavily subsidised by the US long-distance telephone operators who originated almost all calls. The opportunity was created by a change in the heavily regulated relationships which rationed natural levels of contact between Cuba and the USA. When this rationing was relaxed through the deregulation of US law in 1992, Etecsa had a regulated monopoly for charging access fees to Cuban telephone receivers. Its monopoly was enhanced by international telecommunications treaty regulations which created a massive subsidy from the access costs borne by AT&T, MCI and Sprint. The strategy for exploiting this opportunity only unravelled when the resources underpinning the strategy – convertible Mexican peso revenues from other group operations – were devalued in the 1994 collapse of the Mexican economy. In order to continue to access the dollar resources for its Cuban investment, Grupo Domos had to restructure its corporate structure by divesting underlying assets. Structure seems to follow strategy in this case, but it is driven by financial arbitrage opportunities arising from regulatory differences, rather than any diversification strategy.

Reflection

Consider once more an organisation you are familiar with. To what extent is its corporate strategy or structure influenced by a regulatory framework? Does the organisation's management see the regulatory framework as an opportunity or a constraint on its actions, and do you agree with management's assessment?

Changes in regulation create their own opportunities. Are there any impending changes in regulations which might significantly alter the organisation's corporate strategy or structure?

4.2.2 Government interest and corporate strategy

It is also common to encounter corporations whose strategy is inextricably intertwined with government policy and national interest. Recall, for example, the Airbus mini-case from Book 2. A similar situation exists with the entry of the Indonesian government-owned Industri Pesawat Terbang Nusantara into the already overcrowded regional 'commuter' aircraft manufacturing industry. At a time when Fokker in the Netherlands was bankrupt and British Aerospace was trying to withdraw from this market, IPTN launched its first aircraft, the N-250. This was designed to compete against long-established manufacturers such as Canada's Bombardier and Sweden's Saab. IPTN is run by Indonesia's Research and Technology Minister, B.J. Habibie (a long-time friend of President Suharto), who first expressed his intention to create an Indonesian aircraft industry on his appointment to government in 1974.

There are many other examples of the alignment of state interest with large corporations:
- The Venezuelan national oil company has aggressively integrated forwards into US gasoline retailing through its Citgo stations. Given the maturity and fierce competition in this market, this strategy is probably

best seen as state action to secure and control end-product outlets for critical national raw materials in an era of global over-supply.

- Many countries nationalise industries such as steel, coal, airlines and railways. For much of their life European corporations such as Deutsche Telekom, SNCF, British Steel, and INI gained their legal status from statute and legislation, rather than from the commercial law which normally governs commercial corporations.

It is thus not always possible to see the corporation, its strategy or structure, as independent from government policy or regulation. Grupo Domos illustrated both the strategic opportunities and the difficulties that arise from changes in government regulation, while corporations such as IPTN and Citgo are to a greater or lesser extent pursuing the policy of their governments.

4.2.3 The evolution of corporations in alternative economic and social contexts

Chandler's work (1962) on the divisionalised corporation was based on US firms in the early part of the twentieth century. His thesis was that the divisionalised corporation evolved as a result of the diversification and growth strategies of large companies. His work was replicated, with similar results, in the UK (Channon, 1973). The corporations described by Chandler and Channon evolved in relatively stable societies, with well-developed capital markets, where diversification seemed an appropriate strategy for continuing growth. However, corporations evolving in different social and economic conditions may evolve differently. The mini-case on Russia's emerging conglomerate corporations demonstrates a different evolution.

MINI-CASE: RUSSIA'S EMERGING CONGLOMERATE CORPORATIONS 1991–96

In the five years from 1991 to 1996, numerous economic reforms had been introduced in Russia, although market reform was less sweeping than in Hungary, Poland or the Czech Republic. High inflation destroyed much of the value of savings and the spending power of those on fixed incomes. State ownership of industry and commercial enterprise in Russia declined from a virtual 100 per cent to about 30 per cent. Huge slices of the economy, including most state-owned oil, gas, forest products, mining and real estate assets were privatised. Often these were acquired by emerging financial–industrial conglomerates. The six largest of these conglomerates, their interests and connections are described in Table 4.1 opposite.

These conglomerates were diverse, but almost all were built around a mix of cash-generating industrial concerns, investment opportunities in other industries, and a financial institution or bank which could provide or channel the cash to acquire stakes in state industries to be privatised. Almost all of these conglomerates were associated with one of the competing political interests attempting to control the country in this period; the typical Russian 'biznesman' had a 'dyadya', or political patron, to protect their interests. Many of the conglomerates had benefited from tax concessions, duty exemptions, and protective tariffs.

Table 4.1 Russian financial–industrial conglomerates in 1996

Group	Industrial holdings	Political patrons
Oneximbank	Most powerful group with 38% of Norilsk Nickel, 26% of jet engine maker Perm Motors, 26% of auto maker Zil, plus oil, metallurgy and real estate interests	Tightly linked to Kremlin
Menatep	Most diversified of the conglomerates, with 78% of oil giant Yukos, plus controlling interests in plastics, metallurgy, textiles, chemicals, and food-processing companies	Close to former Communist apparatchiks
Alfa	Big player in Moscow region, with interests in real estate, securities trading, cement, candy and chemicals industries	Lacked good connections at national level
Rossiskaya Metallurgia	Controversial group created by Kremlin decree, linking 14 institutes and troubled plants producing steel, alloys, and other metals	Deputy Prime Minister Oleg Soskovets
Most Group	Active in Moscow, with interests spread across banking, real estate, government, construction, television network NTV, and the influential daily newspaper *Today*	Close ties with Moscow Mayor Yuri Luzhkov
Gazprom/ Lukoil/ Imperial Bank	Very powerful but loosely tied limited group. Russia's gas monopoly, its largest oil company, and their jointly owned bank. A big exporter, with Gazprom supplying gas to Europe and Lukoil in oil deals in Libya and the Persian Gulf	Prime Minister Viktor Chernomyrdin

Source of data: International Business Week, *1 April 1996*

In building these conglomerates, a number of strategies were reasonably common:

- Access to cash at an early stage in the reform period. (Oneximbank was created in 1993 through the merger of cash-rich former Soviet trade associations.)
- Acquiring a banking licence or financial institution to mediate financial transactions. (Menatep's communist party connections helped it to gain one of the first private banking licences under Mikhail Gorbachev's *perestroika* reforms in 1988.)
- Using cash to acquire stakes in privatised industries which could be run to generate further cash for further expansion, even when they were highly inefficient by international standards (as in the oil industry).
- Controlling a high percentage of Russia's foreign currency transactions through the export sales of raw materials such as oil and gas.
- Operating private security forces of former members of the Russian army and the KGB security police, to fight off the Mafia for control of their operations.
- Links to political patrons, cheap loans to the government in exchange for access to privatisation stakes, and financing political parties. Political risk was often diversified by funding a variety of political parties.

(*Sources:* International Business Week, *1 April 1996*; Rudloff, 1995)

Russia's emerging conglomerates were mixed financial and industrial corporate structures. They faced strategic issues very different from General Motors, DuPont, Sears and Exxon in the US in the early twentieth century:

1   Opportunism was the rationale for diversification.
2   Since a stable financial market did not exist, an internal bank was essential to the Russian conglomerates' ability to finance operations.
3   Lack of an efficient capital market for either investing or borrowing led the drive to control cash-generating subsidiaries such as oil and gas companies.
4   Corporate strategy was driven by efforts to control stable sources of hard currencies.
5   Tangible property assets (such as real estate, oil and gas properties, mines and forests) were an important hedge against rapid inflation.
6   Social, economic and political instability led to corporate strategies reliant on political patronage.

The Russian conglomerates' corporate strategies, structures and portfolio management had little to do with resolving the opposing tensions of strategic control and managerial freedom in a diversified corporation. Their evolution appears driven more by opportunism, driven in turn by extreme political and financial instability and the lack of a supporting legal, financial and economic infrastructure.

4.2.4 National norms and corporate strategy: financiers and families

Book 3 argued that corporations must try to understand the values and norms which underpin competitors' strategies. As might be expected, there are differences in the ways in which corporations are organised which derive from national or cultural institutional frameworks.

The stock markets of the UK and USA, for example, encourage a market-orientated relationship between shareholders and corporations. Many UK and US corporations have sought to mirror this in the creation of internal capital markets within their divisionalised structures. Albert (1991) distinguishes this model of capitalism from what he calls 'Rhineland' capitalism, common in Germany, Austria, Switzerland and Scandinavia. Banks play a dominant role in providing long-term loan and equity finance in the Rhenish model, sitting on the boards of companies with which they are involved. For example, Deutsche Bank has held an interest in Daimler-Benz since the 1920s, and in 1996 still held nearly 30 per cent of Daimler-Benz equity. State institutions support this alternative model of capitalism. German law, for example, allows pension funds to reinvest a large proportion of employee pensions in company shares, providing a ready source of cheap, friendly capital.

Benefits of the Rhenish model are perceived as a consensual approach to stakeholders (employees and trade unions sitting on the supervisory boards of German companies), and the long time horizon ('long-termism') supposedly implicit in its arrangements for channelling capital. Benefits of the 'Anglo' model are seen as efficient capital markets (encouraging 'rational' investment decisions), allowing a market in corporate control which encourages managerial effectiveness. Supporters of the Rhenish model point to the growing competitiveness of Germany in the 1970s and 1980s as justification for the superiority of that system, while the 'Anglos' point to the dramatic renaissance of US competitiveness, and the simultaneous decline in German productivity, in the early 1990s to support their model.

Clear differences also exist between the structure of Japanese corporations and those in Europe and the USA. Whittington (1993) remarks that Japan appears, at first sight, to have the same multidivisional corporations as those found by Chandler in the United States. Indeed, Mitsubishi placed its mining, shipbuilding and banking subsidiaries in independent profit centres with managerial and investment autonomy in 1908, some years before the divisionalisation of General Motors in the United States. However, this ignores the origins of corporations such as Mitsui and Mitsubishi in the diversified, family-controlled *zaibatsu* merchant houses of the seventeenth century. The *zaibatsu* developed semi-autonomous subsidiaries in the 19th century, not to achieve efficient managerial control, but to allow subsidiaries to raise up to 49 per cent of their capital externally, while retaining overall control in the family.

Since 1945, the *zaibatsu* have evolved into the looser *keiretsu* form, exemplified by firms such as Sumitomo. As in the Rhenish model, *keiretsu* members are interconnected through financial support from *keiretsu* banks. There is heavy trading among members, and interlocking minority shareholdings. These relationships make the *keiretsu* very stable and closed to hostile acquisition (again like the Rhenish model). Unlike US conglomerates they have no central holding company or board of directors:

> What ultimately defines the identities of these groups is membership of their 'Friday clubs', which bring together the presidents of the affiliates regularly for informal co-ordination and mutual support (Dore, 1983). Thus the modern Keiretsu does not rely simply on ownership, markets or debt for control, as in American corporations, but on stable sets of preferential, obligated relationships.
>
> *(Whittington, 1993, p. 121)*

The *keiretsu* may be better understood as 'network' corporations, which we will discuss more fully in Section 5. They are typical of a system of enterprise that Gerlach (1992) has called 'alliance capitalism':

> The essence of alliance capitalism is the strategic forging of long-term intercorporate relationships across a broad spectrum of markets.... These networks of relations are most evident when they become institutionalised into identifiable keiretsu, or industrial groupings. The keiretsu are of two distinct, though overlapping, types. The vertical keiretsu organize suppliers and distribution outlets hierarchically beneath a large, industry-specific manufacturing concern. Toyota Motors' chain of upstream component suppliers is a well-known example of this form of vertical interfirm organisation. These large manufacturers are in turn often clustered within groupings involving trading companies and large banks and insurance companies. These ... 'inter-market keiretsu' (Gerlach, 1992) provide for their members reliable sources of loan capital and a stable core of long-term shareholders. Moreover, like the vertical keiretsu, they establish a partially internalised market in intermediate products.
>
> *(Gerlach and Lincoln, 1992, p. 493)*

An example of a typical *keiretsu*, demonstrating its network nature, is shown in Figure 4.1 overleaf.

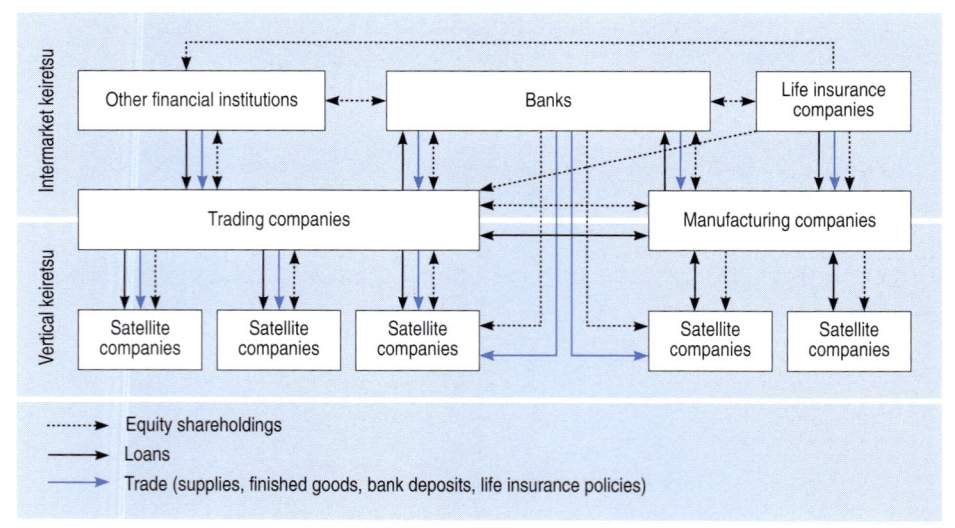

Figure 4.1 Debt, equity, and trade linkages in the vertical and intermarket *keiretsu* (Gerlach, 1992, p. 5)

Korean *chaebol*, such as Daewoo, Samsung, LG (Lucky Goldstar) and Hyundai, share a similar structure to the Japanese *keiretsu*. The development of this type of corporation in culturally different Korea may stem partly from the Japanese imposition of *zaibatsu* forms during its long military occupation of Korea between 1902 and 1945, and partly from the influence of Japan as Korea's main trading partner during its post-1945 industrialisation period.

4.2.5 Alternative corporate strategies and structures

The development of the divisionalised corporation in the United States and its significance in the theory and practice of corporate strategy should be understood alongside other regulatory, governmental, socio-economic, and cultural contexts that have had a big impact on corporate strategies and structures.

Reflection

Think of the organisations with which you do business or compete. You will almost certainly be able to identify European, American, Japanese, Korean, African or Latin American corporations. Your list is likely to include government departments, agencies or regulatory authorities; perhaps you have to liaise with European Union authorities. The corporate strategy and structure of these organisations will inevitably differ because of the varying contexts which influence them. A sensitivity to those contexts goes hand in hand with the lessons of corporate theory.

4.3 TOOLS FOR THE STRATEGY MANAGER

'[The multidivisional structure] removed the executives responsible for the destiny of the entire enterprise from the more routine operational activities and so gave them the time, information, and even psychological commitment for long-term planning and appraisal' (Chandler, 1962, p. 309). It is these general managers, freed from operating responsibilities, who have generated most of the demand for methods of formulating and evaluating business strategies and for concepts of corporate strategy that can lend coherence and meaning to their jobs.

Moreover, neither the corporate structures nor the intellectual paradigms adopted by senior managers have remained static. From the end of the Second World War through to the mid-1980s, there was a clear trend towards pushing responsibility for strategy to lower levels and for elaborating the hierarchy of general managers involved in the strategic process....

This trend was driven, in part, by increasing diversity and size, but it was also driven by the intellectual toolkit of the times – strategic business units, management by objectives, portfolio planning, etc. These tools and management techniques achieved great clarity by isolating each business from others. With minimal interconnections among businesses and few shared resources, planning was simplified and the responsibility for results unambiguously pinpointed....

But this clarity was purchased at a cost. Perhaps most costly were the lost opportunities for co-ordination and resource sharing. For co-ordination – across functions, across regions, across products and across time periods – is at the heart of strategic advantage. The clarity of measurement achieved by extreme profit-centre decentralization also reduced the gains from scale and scope in particular functions and technologies, [and] reduced the coherence of the corporation as a whole....

(Rumelt, 1994, p. xviii)

Rumelt lays out an agenda for our discussion in the next sub-section. We have noted that the development of the divisionalised corporation effectively created the practice of corporate management. The availability of time and information to allow a cycle of planning and control to take place, and the ability to conceive of a large, diverse group of businesses as a simple, clear corporate structure, were reinforced by the corporate managers' identification with the significance of their task for the future of the 'entire enterprise'. A portfolio of corporate management roles and a toolkit of techniques evolved alongside the structures.

4.3.1 The role of corporate management

You should now read Chapter 16 of the Set Book. You may skip over the sections on 'Managing the corporate portfolio' and 'The structure of the multibusiness company' which you read earlier in this book.

Rumelt emphasises the weakness of the multidivisional corporation in the strategic co-ordination of its businesses, at the start of Section 4.3. It is a serious problem. If corporate strategy is fundamentally about the pursuit of superior performance through the combination of disparate businesses, 'extreme decentralisation' is likely to cause problems in realising synergistic benefits or economies of scope.

Portfolio management represented a first attempt to reconcile these problems. It allowed the benefits of a clear, simple multidivisional structure *and* the complementary financial benefits of corporate cash-flow management. When, however, a corporation seeks combination benefits beyond mere financial complement effects, the problem of co-ordination reappears. How can the combination benefits of a core competencies strategy, for example, be achieved in a decentralised multidivisional structure? This brings into question the role of a corporate headquarters.

Grant (pp. 393–413) identifies the ability of corporate management to add value as falling into three categories: managing the corporate portfolio, managing individual businesses and managing internal linkages. The combination benefits of a corporation managing individual businesses stem from the application of common management skills and capabilities across a range of businesses. Managing internal linkages, on the other hand, is concerned with maximising value by managing relationships between businesses, ensuring resources and capabilities are shared or transferred to optimum effect.

Most of the concepts you have just encountered in the Set Book also reflect the tension between the decentralisation of strategic decision-making in the divisionalised corporation, and the need for co-ordination by the headquarters. For example, Goold and Campbell's (1987) typology of corporate management styles and different approaches to corporate 'parenting' identifies approaches characterised by different amounts and types of corporate influence. The dilemmas managers face between centralisation and decentralisation, integration and independence, and control, co-ordination and collaboration are central issues when considering the form of all organisations (as we discussed in Book 8). They are at the heart of recent attempts to change the structure, systems and culture of the CIA described in the following mini-case.

4.3.2 Corporate management: managing structural tensions

MINI-CASE: CHANGE IN THE US CENTRAL INTELLIGENCE AGENCY (CIA)

The CIA has for many years been characterised by extreme decentralisation. The Agency has been structured as four separate directorates: Intelligence, Operations, Science and Technology, and Administration. The directorates are sub-divided into geographic offices with considerable autonomy. For example, the Intelligence directorate had ten geographic offices. This decentralisation and autonomy meant that co-ordinating intelligence operations was extremely complex. In the Bosnian conflict, for example, intelligence-gathering involved up to six separate offices.

The culture of secrecy that surrounded its activities permeated its management, and directorates fiercely guarded their independence and management systems. The agency, in turn, was believed to obscure its activities from the audit of the US congress. This secrecy and decentralisation had been largely accepted when national security had been under threat, and generous defence budgets obscured the resulting organisational slack. In the 1990s, however, important changes occurred:

1. The security threat from the Soviet Union that had dominated US foreign policy since 1945 diminished significantly with the Soviet collapse in 1991.

2. Pressure grew to address the problem of the national budget deficit; the size of the budget previously allocated to counter the Soviet threat provided obvious targets for reductions.

3. The CIA had successfully resisted attempts to make it accountable to politicians. With the reduced security threat, its grounds for resisting Congressional oversight disappeared.

4. The trial of Aldrich H. Ames, who had sold CIA information to Soviet authorities over many years, revealed the worst US security breach since

1945. The CIA culture of secrecy and autonomy had prevented concerns about Ames being pursued earlier. Morale was severely weakened.

These circumstances led to the agency redefining its business, from countering the Soviet threat to defeating terrorism and criminal activities such as narcotics trafficking. This change of strategy brought them into competition with the police and internal security forces, and combined with pressures for accountability to Congress, an end to secrecy, and value for money in management, to render obsolete the old corporate structure of extreme decentralisation and duplication of effort.

A new Director [Deutch] of the CIA was appointed in 1994, accountable to the president and Congress for a $3 billion budget and 17,000 widely dispersed employees. Deutch, in turn, appointed Nora Slatkin from the Defense Department as executive director to manage the agency's activities. While Deutch concentrated on managing the relationships with the main stakeholders, Slatkin set about changing the CIA:

- Directorates are to produce five-year plans and budgets for the first time. These are scrutinised for any activity which does not match the new anti-terrorism and drugs mission.
- New sex discrimination procedures have been put in place following the settlement of damaging law suits arising from allegations of female employees.
- Disciplinary panels have begun to punish irregular covert practices.
- A Human Resources Oversight Council has been set up and recruiting is now centralised. Directorates and geographic offices previously operated independent personnel systems.
- Grounds of national security are no longer used to displace normal management practice such as career development and performance-linked reward programmes.

(Adapted from International Business Week, 26 February 1996)

Activity 4.1

Having read the CIA mini-case, what do you see as the main objectives of the shift to a more centralised corporate strategy and structure?

What are the likely constraints or limitations on greater control at the corporate level?

Discussion

The centralisation strategy must be set against the following: Slatkin lacks spying experience; geographic dispersion remains unavoidable for the agency; morale is still low from the Ames case.

The CIA is in direct competition with other security agencies for funding. Cost-consciousness and reduced national security requirements make the elimination of duplication and greater co-ordination of activities essential. The mini-case says little of the operational or structural changes necessary to achieve greater co-ordination.

Greater co-ordination, control and accountability risk losing sight of the main drivers of intelligence operations: operatives' ability to protect and nurture their sources of information. Where the penalties for discovery may involve death, professional operatives need the power to organise their own activities. Centralisation must therefore co-exist with high degrees of autonomy, which clash with the need to co-ordinate and control. The agency's core competence involves competing for scarce intelligence-gathering and analytical resources, and they are attempting to leverage these into different end-product markets. However, since these new end-product markets have similar characteristics to the previous ones, the CIA is likely to need to develop more sophisticated forms of co-ordination and network management, rather than simply increasing centralisation. We consider these issues further in Section 5.

5 Networks and Corporations

One way of making sense of the tensions between centralisation and decentralisation is to accept them. Sloan (1963, pp. 53 and 57) enunciated two guiding principles for managing the divisionalised structure at General Motors:

1. The responsibility attached to a chief executive of each operation shall in no way be limited. Each such organisation ... shall be complete in every necessary function and enable[d] to exercise its full initiative and logical development.

2. Certain central organization functions are absolutely essential to the logical development and proper control of the Corporation's activities.

On reflection, he also recognised the crucial importance of the ambiguity that lay at the heart of his two principles:

> I am amused to see that the language is contradictory, and that its very contradiction is the crux of the matter.... The language of organisation has always suffered some want of words to express the true facts and circumstances of human interaction. One usually asserts one aspect or another of it at different times, such as the absolute independence of the part, and again the need for co-ordination, and again the concept of the whole with a guiding centre.
>
> *(Sloan, 1963, p. 58)*

It is increasingly obvious, in strategic terms, that the need (as Sloan's comments suggest) is to get away from the polarisation of centralisation or decentralisation, autonomy or control. The CIA mini-case shows that looser structural forms may now be needed. Book 8 considered some of the issues behind this search for structural flexibility in managing corporations. We have already examined the Japanese *keiretsu* form in Section 4, and we noted that it had network features. In this section, we will go on to examine networks more closely, and evaluate how networks might help in resolving some of these tensions inherent in corporate strategy and management.

5.1 Networks and Institutional Frameworks

> The prevalence of network organizations in the Japanese economy poses a formidable challenge to western economic theories that view hierarchical organization (government or corporate) and atomized markets as the polar twin mechanisms through which transactions in an advanced economy take place.... Yet the alternative to formal hierarchy in Japan is not impersonal arm's-length markets, but informal networks based on trust and long-term 'relational contracting'.... Like the myriad other ties that thread through the Japanese economy, they have an enduring, obligatory, and co-operative character that economic models of efficient markets fail to capture.
>
> *(Gerlach and Lincoln, 1992, pp. 494–5)*

5.1.1 Networks in the Asian institutional context

In Book 4 we considered transaction cost economics (Williamson, 1975) and noted that it can be used to evaluate where the boundaries of an organisation may best be set. The principal strategic choice of transaction costing was 'make or buy'. This theory was also used earlier in this book: diversifications or divestments represent decisions to achieve combination benefits either through external trading (market transactions) or through internal interactions (corporate combinations).

While useful in many ways, this simple choice of make or buy does little to explain Asian networks or the growing popularity of such forms in Europe and America. One criticism of network structures in Asian countries is that the networks of Japan, Korea or China contain market imperfections which prevent the free flow of information and capital.

Activity 5.1

You may remember the discussion of Asian institutions and network corporations in the Course Reader article for Book 9 by Biggart and Hamilton (1992). Review your notes from the article, or refresh your memory of it. How do these authors explain Asian corporate structures?

Discussion

The authors draw a picture of Western societies and organisations encouraging autonomous, independent action throughout their social, legal and ethical structures. The authors explain the interfirm networks of Asia as a result of an alternative 'institutional' framework, a model of capitalism founded on social relationships and interaction, rather than the autonomy and individual independence of Anglo-American models of capitalism.

This debate about Asian and Anglo institutional structures and the values which support them is held against a continually shifting map of international and economic ebbs and flows. After the 'Asian miracle' of the 1960s, '70s and '80s we can see the period between 1991 and 1995 as one where both the Japanese and the German economies were stagnant, and the US and UK economies made significant competitiveness gains.

> ... some of the ideas that seemed compelling to policy intellectuals at the beginning of the 1990s look fairly silly now. Above all, the Japan of late 1995 – its economy dead in the water for the fifth straight year, its financial system in the red on a scale that makes America's thrift crisis look small, and even its vaunted semiconductor industry in retreat as a resurgent Silicon Valley attacks from above, while Korea attacks from below – hardly looks like the sleek, sinister technological superpower of legend. Still, fear of Japan has become institutionalised; too many people have based their careers on the Japanese threat for them to admit that this threat is not what it used to be – and perhaps never was.
>
> (Krugman, 1995, p. 111)

The point made by Biggart and Hamilton, however, is that Asian networks should be understood properly as an alternative model, rather than as necessarily a superior model.

5.1.2 Networks in alternative institutional frameworks

This discussion so far has implied a norm whereby networks based on social relationships are the prevalent corporate structure in Asian economies, whilst Anglo economies base economic activity on a belief in market transactions and individualistic personal and organisational behaviour.

These Anglo and Asian stereotypes, while helpful in identifying the existence of network structures, are ultimately restrictive. You have already met Kay's (1993) classification of co-operative 'relational contracting' as an alternative to classical and spot-market contracting in Book 2. Kay gives many non-Asian examples of relational contracting. Examples of successful network structures in non-Asian contexts include:

- the network of Italian suppliers and global collaborators used by Benetton (mini-case in Book 4)
- professional service firms such as accountants, lawyers and management consultants, who have long structured themselves as flexible associations of professionals with complementary skills or locations.

Neither is it true that all Asian corporations remain networks. Deep recession and high exchange rates in Japan in the early 1990s have led some Japanese corporations to change. Fujitsu, for example, have adopted policies which go against our expectations of the 'social relationship' model:

- Nearly 10 per cent of Fujitsu's Japanese workforce has been cut since 1991, including some redundancies.
- The group has adopted a 'flatter' management structure and linked pay and promotion more to individual performance, rather than length of service.
- Fujitsu has broken a number of long-term supply arrangements with Japanese suppliers, switching to US and south-east Asian suppliers, offering price reductions of up to 30 per cent.

These examples indicate that the institutionalised stereotypes of theory are neither fixed in time nor clear-cut in practice.

5.1.3 Drivers towards forming networks and alliances

Gomes-Cassares (1996) is more specific. His study of bilateral alliances and network 'constellations' in high-technology sectors suggests that rapid change, complexity and uncertainty favour the development of networks in preference to single-unit corporations. The study included US, European and Japanese companies in advanced technology sectors operating in globalising markets. He saw four main drivers which might encourage the formation of networks rather than single-firm corporations:

1. *Rising global competition* – Networks and alliances can allow cost to be spread over larger volumes, give access to skills and assets in different countries, and overcome regulatory barriers.
2. *Deepening industry convergence* – Networks allow leading companies from traditional industries to exploit new opportunities arising from convergence, by allowing faster access to complementary skills.

3 *Battles over technical standards* – In an emerging industry, users adopting any one competing standard may be influenced by alliances or networks of collaborating competitors.

4 *Positioning* – Diversification or repositioning may be helped by membership of a network or alliance.

The growth of network structures may therefore be a reflection of some of the strong general influences on trade which will be discussed in the international context in Book 11.

5.2 THE DISTINCTIVENESS OF NETWORKS

If certain factors are driving the formation of networks and alliances rather than single-firm corporations, the different forms they take, and any advantages that can come from organising commercial activities as networks, need to be understood.

5.2.1 Networks, boundaries and control

We need to revisit some of our notions concerning the corporation, adopting a more fluid view of organisational boundaries. More fundamentally, we need to expand the range of strategic options from 'make or buy' to 'make, buy or co-operate'.

Another critical corporate strategy consideration concerns the way in which networks shift the emphasis of corporate management from internal control to network co-ordination. One of the main advantages of the single corporation over a network or alliance is its 'unified control' (Gomes-Cassares, 1996). Co-ordinated joint decision-making rather than full control is at the very heart of network and alliance strategies, however, and this may itself be a source of advantage. Gomes-Cassares identifies two main methods used by networks and alliances to ensure that participants fulfil their obligations:

1 *Establishing group norms and standards* – Network norms and standards need to be distinct from individual member company norms.

2 *Leadership in group decision-making* – Consistent strategy requires joint decision-making involving a network leader, or an agreed method of making decisions by compromise or consensus.

These issues of boundary management and control mechanisms are at the heart of effective network organisations:

> But to focus on the 'boundary-marker' role of alliances is to mistake the trees for the forest. The common definition of a clear boundary is one that separates territories; a blurry boundary, it follows, is one that joins these territories to some degree. The tighter the collaboration between two firms – that is, the blurrier the boundary between them – the more the firms will in effect be joined and the more they will wield economic power as a unit. Unless the alliance changes into a full merger, this unification of power is never complete. But the actions of these firms will still be co-ordinated to some extent. ...
>
> Single firms and constellations are different organisational units with the same purpose: to control a set of capabilities so as to maximise their return. The control systems of these units differ substantially, as do the

way units combine and upgrade their capabilities. In a given competitive context, these differences give one organisational form or the other an advantage.

(Gomes-Cassares, 1996, pp. 3–5)

5.2.2 Networks and competition

Traditionally, collaboration by firms has been frowned on by economists as the basis for monopolies and cartels. However, the fashion for alliances and network collaborations seems to be generating sophisticated new ways to compete and additional sources of advantage over traditional firms.

Potential sources of advantage for networks derive from the following (Gomes-Cassares, 1996):

- *Flexible capabilities* – Networks can be better equipped to assemble, manage and upgrade a diverse, and hence unique, set of capabilities. The possibilities for innovative combination of these capabilities are greater than those available to a single firm.
- *Specialisation and the division of labour* – Just as a factory can achieve better productivity by dividing its production tasks, so networks can benefit from allowing members to specialise and better develop their own capabilities.
- *Learning* – In Book 4 we described organisations as bundles of capabilities, and characterised them as relatively fixed in the short term, and slow to change. The path dependences of capability development, however, can be overcome by the creation of new alliances or by inviting a new member to join a network.
- *Increased options* – In situations where the direction of change is uncertain, alliances and networks can be a rich source of strategic options, for a limited commitment of resources.

The advantages alliances and networks may provide are essentially corporate combination benefits based on combinations of capabilities to provide synergies. This echoes advantage based on combinations of distinctive capabilities at business strategy level.

It is important, however, to indicate clearly that networks are complex structures and, as such, are complex to manage. They require co-ordination and negotiation skills which many managements do not possess and have to work hard to develop. Networks are not panaceas or substitutes for effective management practice. Just as with potential synergy benefits, many network benefits may never be realised by some organisations, or at least only after extensive investments of time and other resources.

More of the practical detail of managing networks and alliances, and co-operative strategies, will be addressed in Book 11.

5.2.3 Networks as combinations of capabilities

One area of business activity where network structures are common is the biotechnology sector, which you encountered in Book 6. Here networks provide a critical means for separate organisations to combine the complementary capabilities necessary to compete (see the mini-case below).

MINI-CASE: BIOTECHNOLOGY NETWORKS

Major breakthroughs in the commercial application of biotechnology came in 1973 at Stanford and California Universities, and, in 1975, under the auspices of the British Medical Research Council. The former developed the technique of 'recombinant DNA', which has subsequently been used to manufacture growth hormones, interferon, and human insulin. The latter developed a 'monoclonal' technique for producing specific antibodies at low cost, a technology which has been used to produce vaccines.

After the US Patents Office granted the two universities rights to exploit their recombinant DNA techniques in 1976, a number of biotechnology ventures were set up by universities and scientists with expertise in the area, in collaboration with entrepreneurs and financiers. These ventures were initially funded primarily by venture capitalists, although public offerings of shares were made to receptive markets in the early 1980s. (Genentech offered its shares at $35 in 1980, only to see the price bid up to $89 within an hour of trading opening.)

By the mid-1980s, however, the excitement of this new sector waned as it became clear that venture capitalists, used to seeing a return on investment within a few years, would have to wait considerably longer to make returns from biotechnology. At this stage, an underlying tendency for biotechnology to be organised as a network of alliances asserted itself. This appears to arise from two main factors:

1. The commercial applications of the research and core techniques were varied and spanned many interests and sectors, cutting across traditional industry boundaries.

2. The biotechnology firms set up by universities and scientists were involved in basic and applied research. They did not have skills for clinically testing and developing prototypes, for dealing with regulatory approval bodies, or for producing and marketing commercial products. Neither did they need these skills, as they were able to capture the value of their core techniques and capabilities in the rights to the research they carried out prior to development. The capabilities which biotechnology firms lacked were already available in established industry-specific corporations.

These factors led to the development of a web of alliances, as corporations from different industries happily collaborated to fund research into core biotechnology techniques. On the one hand, biotechnology firms (such as Biogen, Genentech and Centocor), research universities (such as MIT, Stanford and California), and research institutes (such as The Whitehead) acted as brokers for the knowledge derived from basic and applied research; on the other, the exploitation of discoveries depended on the development, production and marketing skills of corporations drawn from a variety of industries (for example, Shell, Corning Glass and Monsanto). The latter were also important as a source of funds for the research companies at a time when venture capital dwindled.

(Sources: Barley et al., 1992; Powell and Brantley, 1992)

The biotechnology sector lends itself to analysis using the core competencies framework we discussed in Section 2 and the four sources of advantage given at the beginning of this section. The networks that have grown up utilise the core competencies of each type of member organisation. The main research firms and universities have core competencies in biotechnology research, leading to the development of core products. To develop and market end products, however, they ally themselves to other corporations with these competencies. The networks provide the firms with an efficient means for leveraging core competencies and core products across a variety of distinct end-product markets. Thus, the networks extend naturally to cover pharmaceuticals, chemicals, health care, waste management and agriculture corporations.

The different members of the networks are dependent on each other for access to their respective competencies. In addition, co-operative behaviour is encouraged by the long-term nature of biotechnology; all partners continue to be dependent on each other on an ongoing basis; and, as with most research, the precise outcomes of projects cannot be determined in advance. Relational contracting behaviours are, therefore, more appropriate and encourage the persistence of the networks.

Although the innovations of commercial biotechnology have spawned many new applications and products, and given birth to a specialist biotechnology research industry, they have not (at the time of writing) broken down existing industry barriers in the pharmaceuticals, health care, agricultural, chemical, waste management and energy sectors. In 1996 one of the large end-product organisations, the chemicals and pharmaceuticals corporation Monsanto, decided to focus all future activities specifically on biotechnology applications in its industries.

Compare that with a sector where innovation appears to be leading to a blurring of traditional industry boundaries: the 'convergence' of media, information systems and telecommunications in the development of new interactive and on-line entertainment, computing and communications services, such as home shopping, video-on-demand and the Internet. This multimedia sector (or sectors) appears to exhibit at least three of Gomes-Cassares drivers for network collaboration: rising global competition, deepening industry convergence, and (prospective) battles over technical standards. The sector is examined in the video 'The Information Superhighway'.

You should now watch video VC 0865 band 1, after first reading the accompanying audio-visual notes.

5.2.4 The place of networks in corporate strategy

Networks are structures to exploit the combination benefits of corporate strategy, just as traditional multibusiness corporations are. Corporate strategy is about achieving superior performance from combining disparate activities. The range of combination benefits available from networks may be greater and wider than those available to corporations: increased possibilities from any number of collaborations; increased strategic moves available to members of networks. The clear disadvantages of networks are the loss of direct control and clarity. Although the experience of Asian networks and the relational contracting principles they follow suggests these disadvantages can be overcome, they require most 'Anglo' and Western corporations to reinvent themselves.

6 Summary and Conclusion

Corporate strategy is concerned with making sense of some of the most important strategy innovations that have occurred in twentieth-century business – innovations such as the multidivisional corporation, growth through diversification, and portfolio strategies. Theory often lags behind practice in business research, and the study of corporate strategy is no different. The problem for the innovators of these corporate strategy techniques is that as the workings of their innovations are eventually understood, so they have been copied and any advantage from innovation has dissipated.

As researchers have better explained and communicated ideas such as the multidivisional corporation, so their shortcomings and unresolved tensions (such as the balance between centralisation and decentralisation) have also become more apparent. Solutions such as portfolio strategies seem less ideal now than they did twenty years ago. At the same time, researchers have increasingly looked beyond the borders of Anglo-American business practice and identified practices that have evolved in alternative institutional, cultural and socio-economic environments, such as the network corporations of Asia. Broadening our horizons to better understand alternative approaches to corporate strategy would seem to be essential if business is becoming more complex, volatile and global in nature.

What is emerging in this field is a concern with understanding the benefits that can be achieved from combining the distinct capabilities of a corporation's businesses to the best effect. No longer are synergies commonly expressed as the benefits of combining product and market opportunities. They have shifted from attractive industries to distinctive capabilities, core competencies, sources of advantage and sustainability.

We emerge, therefore, from our study of corporate strategy with a focus on the importance of leveraging core competencies across different business activities to create new corporate value from existing capabilities. We have emphasised the superiority of the synergy benefits that can be obtained from combining invisible assets, as opposed to the complementary benefits of combining physical assets. The difficulty of imitating synergy benefits from invisible assets also means that the superior returns from these are far more likely to persist in the long term.

Finally, we have noted the growing significance of networks in corporate strategy. The network can, of course, be seen as a means to an end, in so far as it allows access to a set of capabilities which are not core. It can, however, also be seen as an end in itself: the distinctiveness that drives advantage can come from the very uniqueness of the combined relationships. In this sense, it may be the purest source of corporate superior performance.

REFERENCES

Albert, M. (1991) *Capitalisme contre Capitalisme*, Seuil, Paris.

Armour, H.O. and Teece, D.J. (1986) 'Organisational structure and economic performance: a test of the multidivisional hypothesis', in Barney and Ouchi, *op. cit.*

Barley, S.R., Freeman, J. and Hybels, R.C. (1992) 'Strategic alliances in commercial biotechnology', in Nohria and Eccles, *op. cit.*

Barney, J.B. and Ouchi, W.G. (1986) *Organisational Economics*, Jossey-Bass, San Francisco.

Biggart, N.W. and Hamilton, G.G. (1992) 'On the limits of a firm-based theory to explain business networks: the western bias of neo-classical economics', in Nohria and Eccles, *op. cit.*

Bogner, W.C. and Thomas, H. (1994) 'Core competence and competitive advantage: a model and illustrative evidence from the pharmaceutical industry', in Hamel and Heene, *op. cit.*

Campbell, A. and Luchs, K.S. (eds) (1992) *Strategic Synergy*, Butterworth-Heinemann, Oxford.

Chandler, A.D. (1962) *Strategy and Structure*, MIT Press, Cambridge, MA.

Channon, D. (1973) *The Strategy and Structure of British Enterprise*, Macmillan, Basingstoke.

Dore, R. (1983) 'Goodwill and the spirit of market capitalism', *British Journal of Sociology*, Vol. 34, pp. 459–82.

Eccles, R.G. and Nohria, N. (1992) *Beyond the Hype*, Harvard Business School Press, Boston, MA.

Gerlach, M.L. (1992) *Alliance Capitalism: the social organisation of Japanese business*, University of California Press, Berkeley, CA.

Gerlach, M.L. and Lincoln, J.R. (1992) 'The organisation of business networks in the United States and Japan', in Nohria and Eccles, *op. cit.*

Gibbs, P. (1993) 'Determinants of corporate restructuring: the relative importance of corporate governance, takeover threat, and free cash flow', *Strategic Management Journal*, Vol. 14, pp. 51–68.

Gomes-Cassares, B. (1996) *The Alliance Revolution*, Harvard University Press, Cambridge, MA.

Goold, M. and Campbell, A. (1987) *Strategies and Styles*, Blackwell, Oxford.

Goold, M. and Luchs, K.S. (eds) (1996) *Managing the Multibusiness Company*, Routledge, London.

Grant, R., Jammine, A. and Thomas, H. (1988) 'Diversity, diversification, and profitability among British manufacturing companies 1972–1984', *Academy of Management Journal*, Vol. 31, pp. 771–801.

Grinyer, P.H., Mayes, D.H. and McKiernan, P. (1988) *Sharpbenders*, Blackwell, Oxford.

Hamel, G. (1994) 'The concept of core competence', in Hamel and Heene, *op. cit.*

Hamel, G. and Heene, A. (1994) *Competence-based Competition*, Wiley, Chichester.

Hamel, G. and Prahalad, C.K. (1994) *Competing for the Future*, Harvard Business School Press, Boston, MA.

Harrigan, K.R. (1988) *Managing Maturing Businesses*, Lexington Books, Lexington, MA.

Itami, H.I. (1992) 'Invisible assets', in Campbell and Luchs, *op. cit.*

Jensen, M.C. and Meckling, W.H. (1976) 'Theory of the firm: managerial behaviour, agency cost, and ownership structure', *Journal of Financial Economics*, Vol. 3, pp. 305–60.

Kay, J. (1993) *Foundations of Corporate Success*, Oxford University Press, Oxford.

Krugman, P. (1995) 'Tripping up world trade', *The World in 1996*, Economist Intelligence Unit, London, pp. 110–11.

Levitt, T. (1960) 'Marketing myopia', *Harvard Business Review*, July/August.

Markowitz, H.M. (1952) 'Portfolio selection', *Journal of Finance*, Vol. 7, pp. 77–91.

Nohria, N. and Eccles, R.G. (eds) (1992) *Networks and Organizations: structure, form and action*, Harvard Business School Press, Boston, MA.

Porter, M.E. (1980) *Competitive Strategy: techniques for analyzing industries and competitors*, The Free Press, New York.

Porter, M.E. (1987) 'From competitive advantage to corporate strategy', *Harvard Business Review*, May/June.

Powell, W.W. and Brantley, P. (1992) 'Competitive cooperation in biotechnology: learning through networks?', in Nohria and Eccles, *op. cit.*

Prahalad, C.K. and Hamel, G. (1990) 'The core competence of the corporation', *Harvard Business Review*, May/June.

Rudloff. H.-J. (1995) 'Will Russia make it?', *The World in 1996*, Economist Intelligence Unit, London, pp. 130–3.

Rumelt, R.P. (1974) *Strategy, Structure, and Economic Performance*, Harvard Business School Press, Boston, MA.

Rumelt, R.P. (1994) 'Foreword', in Hamel and Heene, *op. cit.*

Rumelt, R.P., Schendel, D.E. and Teece, D.J. (1994) *Fundamental Issues in Strategy*, Harvard Business School Press, Boston, MA.

Slatter, S. St P. (1984) *Corporate Recovery*, Penguin, Harmondsworth.

Sloan, A.P. (1963) *My Years with General Motors*, Doubleday, New York.

Whittington, R. (1993) *What is Strategy – and does it matter?*, Routledge, London.

Williamson, O.E. (1975) *Markets and Hierarchies: analysis and antitrust implications*, The Free Press, New York.

Acknowledgements

Grateful acknowledgement is made to the following sources for permission to reproduce material in this book:

Text

Pages 29–30: Grinyer, P.H., Mayes, D.G. and McKiernan, P. 1988, *Sharpbenders*, pp. 232–234, Basil Blackwell Publishers.

Figures

Figure 2.2: Itami, H. 'Invisible assets' in Campbell, A. and Luchs, K.S. (eds) 1992, *Strategic Synergy*, Butterworth-Heinemann Ltd; *Figure 4.1:* Gerlach, M.L. 1992, *Alliance Capitalism: the social organization of Japanese business*, p. 5, University of California Press.

Tables

Table 3.1: Harrigan, R. R. 1988, *Managing Maturing Businesses*, Lexington Books, by permission of D.C. Heath and Company, Inc.; *Table 4.1:* Reprinted from 1 April 1996 issue of *Business Week* by special permission, © 1996 by The McGraw-Hill Companies, Inc.

BOOK 11

INTERNATIONAL STRATEGY: COMPETING ACROSS BORDERS

Author: Susan Segal-Horn

MBA Strategy

Contents

1 **Introduction** — 5
   1.1 Is international strategy different? — 5
   1.2 Overview of the book — 6
   1.3 Learning objectives of this book — 7

2 **International competition: the management of international trade** — 8
   2.1 Traditional and modern factors of production: mobile v. immobile — 10
   2.2 'Advanced' factors of production and the growth of the MNC — 15
   2.3 Types of international strategy — 16
   2.4 The great game: the role of governments and the limits to regulation — 17

3 **Comparative advantage and international competitive advantage** — 21
   3.1 World trade and international competitive advantage — 21
   3.2 Comparative advantage revisited: the Porter 'diamond' — 21
   3.3 Configuration of the international value chain — 28
   3.4 Means and ends: Ghoshal's 'organising framework' — 30
   3.5 Summary — 33

4 **International industries and international firms** — 34
   4.1 Types of international industry — 34
   4.2 Types of international firm — 41
   4.3 International competition in services — 45

5 **International strategy development** — 48
   5.1 Strategic alliances and joint ventures — 48
   5.2 Mergers and acquisitions — 53

6 **Summary and conclusion** — 57

References — 58

Acknowledgements — 61

1 Introduction

International business matters. It matters not only to the planning departments of large multinational companies (MNCs), or to governments trying to attract the investment of such companies to create jobs for their people. It matters also to the managers of small and medium-size firms, and to neighbourhood stores, trying to retain the business of their local customers. Whether they know it or not, they are competing in an international market-place for goods and services. Every initiative taken by an international firm has an impact in a local market and on the market share of local organisations and their ability to satisfy their customers.

To illustrate this point it is interesting to note that, at the time of writing, the latest threat to small retailers comes from the major oil corporations such as Exxon, Shell or BP/Mobil in the development of 'convenience stores' on their gas/petrol station forecourts, which is the fastest-growing new retail sector in the developed economies. It also directly undermines the one competitive advantage of the small local convenience store – that of staying open late. Petrol forecourts are often open 24 hours a day.

Many business decisions are taken in an international context and frequently involve managing across borders. This book will help you understand the development of international trade, the role of multinationals in international trade and how to structure and develop MNCs to meet changes in the international competitive environment. We will discuss what drives international strategy and both the advantages and the problems of implementing strategy internationally, as well as to explain the strategic alternatives open to an organisation when it extends its activities across borders. For both products and services, the activities of the multinational organisation may be seen as an outcome of the interrelationship of industry characteristics, strategic flexibility and organisational capability. This has relevance for all organisations including national and local government, small and medium-sized enterprises, even when they themselves have no activities outside their domestic market nor any plans to develop any in the future. Your organisation may carry out no international activities whatsoever and yet be strongly affected by international trade and the strategies of MNCs. In this sense international strategy affects us all.

1.1 Is International Strategy Different?

Activity 1.1

Consider for a few moments the difference between strategy and international strategy.

Discussion

When an organisation first decides to expand outside its domestic market, it faces a step change in the complexity attached to every business decision. For all organisations, operating internationally is much more challenging than operating solely within their domestic market. In every facet of managerial decision-making it creates greater risks and problems. For example, geographic market selection for international expansion is far more complex than expansion within an organisation's domestic market. Although domestic expansion certainly requires careful judgement of relative market attractiveness, potential competition, adaptation to local market conditions and coping with problems of managing the business over the larger geographic area, challenges of a different order arise with selection of markets for international expansion.

International markets often contain barriers to trade, both tariff and non-tariff, such as import quotas, or rules on foreign ownership. Other obvious but daunting challenges include different laws, different planning regulations, different transportation infrastructure and distribution systems, different languages, different currencies and exchange rates, different consumer preferences and any number of differences in individual and social behaviour, political systems and religious or ethnic norms. As a result, operating internationally involves decisions about how, and to what extent, to adapt products, management and investment plans to take account of these national and cultural differences. All this means fine judgements about degrees of political risk, financial risk and commercial risk in every international business decision, which do not arise within the domestic market.

We cannot stress too strongly at the outset that while all strategic thinking occurs in a dynamic context, developing robust strategies, deliverable across international borders, is the most dynamic and complex context of all.

1.2 OVERVIEW OF THE BOOK

This book draws not only on strategic management research, but also on the fields of organisational behaviour, economics and marketing. Section 2 provides a brief overview of international trade theory in order to explain the theory of comparative advantage and its role in international strategy. This section explains the sources of advantage available to MNCs and the complex relationship between them and governments. Initial definitions of some different types of international strategy are given. It will be stressed that what drives international strategy is the creation of a broader set of strategic options and choices.

Section 3 deals with comparative advantage. It also discusses the configuration and co-ordination of geographically dispersed international value chains and sources of advantage from global, local or 'glocal' strategies. It considers these different international strategies and structures in more detail. An overview of the drivers of globalisation is given in Section 4. It includes cultural homogenisation and the emergence of global markets; the advantages of global operations; the impact of regional trading blocs; whether markets are regional or global; and a range of new organisational structures for complex international strategies, including global, multidomestic and transnational organisations, and their role in different types of international strategies.

This section concludes with a consideration of the problems of service organisations in managing intangible services across borders.

Finally, in Section 5 we examine different modes of international strategy development – the popularity of strategic alliances and the traditional route of mergers and acquisitions. Both provide a means of acquiring instant market share, adding capabilities or resources. Any objective for an alliance may equally well be a reason for a merger or acquisition. They are different means to the same ends. However since the indirect (non-financial) costs of an alliance may be high, this section focuses on the managerial and operational issues in making alliances work effectively.

This book will carry forward strategy frameworks such as the value chain from earlier books, as well as introducing new concepts to help you make sense of the dynamics of international strategy.

1.3 LEARNING OBJECTIVES OF THIS BOOK

After studying this book you should be able to:

- extend the conceptual and analytical tools of strategic management to the formulation and implementation of international strategy
- develop greater understanding of some of the major problems facing managers of international organisations, especially those working within multinational corporations, as well as those organisations competing or doing business with MNCs within national markets
- demonstrate the greater complexity, including both increased opportunities and increased risks, that accompanies international operations
- explore alternative patterns of strategy, structure and operations, appropriate in different international contexts and changing international market conditions.

2 INTERNATIONAL COMPETITION: THE MANAGEMENT OF INTERNATIONAL TRADE

This section introduces a number of themes: modern factors of production; the theory of comparative advantage and its interaction with competitive advantage; how the MNC delivers advantage simply because of what it is; some different types of international trade and international strategy; the role of government in international strategy; and the role of risk in international strategy. We hope to convey why local organisations find it difficult to cope with international competition and the repercussions of international trade and MNC activity on local organisations in their local markets.

As this book proceeds, many of the concepts and models of strategic management that you have already encountered such as resources, value chains or organisation structures and cultures, will be applied to international strategy. We begin with some background about international trade, which should provide a context and a 'map' for our later analysis.

Until the end of the nineteenth century, international trade was dominated by trading companies or investment houses. Since then, international trade has become increasingly dominated by multinational companies. The difference between the former and the latter is that the activities of multinationals are based on foreign direct investment (FDI): locating part of their activities such as design, manufacturing, assembly, sales, distribution or R&D, in other than their home countries. Furthermore, these investments were actively managed as a single operational entity in unified corporations. This has influenced the nature of international trade, since much of it is now internal to these international corporations, carried out between their own business units and operating divisions, either importing goods produced in their overseas subsidiaries, or exporting products to be sold by these subsidiaries. MNCs therefore oversee immense resources and many have assets that exceed those of all but the richest national governments. This means that such firms play an important role not only within their domestic economies, but also in the economies of the many host nations in which they have a presence. It also explains their impact on the conditions of local competition for the small and medium-sized firms within these various national markets. The quality of management in multinational corporations, therefore, has implications far beyond the corporations themselves.

Over time the task of international managers has changed. The early emphasis was on managing large-scale technologies of production and distribution for maximum benefit from scale efficiencies of output. This drove companies to international expansion beyond the domestic market, mainly to develop markets of sufficient size to absorb the new high levels of output and to provide continuity of supply. As already discussed in Book 10, Chandler (1962) described these developments in detail.

However, overseas subsidiaries gradually became more autonomous, often in response to protectionist barriers erected by national governments against foreign exports. The task of managers became the planning, control and administration of large independent overseas operations. From the 1960s onwards, another set of trends began a new pattern of convergence. Gradual economic integration through international trade agreements, the development of international communication and transportation systems and technological advances in products and components, transformed the cost structures of many industries and necessitated a complete rethink of the basic economic assumptions of supply and demand for that industry. It became possible to redesign from first principles the whole chain of activities of production and supply. This rebuilding usually included much broader options for where to locate business activities worldwide, in order to maximise both efficiency-seeking by the firm and responsiveness to shifting patterns of demand in different markets.

The management skills needed in this latest phase of international business are for high levels of integration and co-ordination across borders. That is the capability being emphasised in much current corporate advertising, including that of ABB (Asea Brown Boveri – already met in Book 8) the Swedish/Swiss engineering company. Its 1990s advertising campaigns featured captions such as 'The art of being local worldwide'. This is a rhetoric implying local presence, local roots and local services, combined with international reach and resources, which can be brought to bear for local customers' benefit. (Whether ABB delivered this will be revisited in Section 4.) Such resources do not have to be directly owned by the company but may be available through an alliance or partnership with another firm. The rapid growth of co-operative ventures as a common feature of international business means that international managers at most levels must have the ability to adapt and learn from collaboration, as well as from competition, to be effective in the changing world arena.

Activity 2.1

Why do you think the assertion is being made that an understanding of international strategy is just as relevant for small and medium-sized enterprises as it is for the managers of multinationals? Try to think of one or two examples of this. Is the assertion true for not-for-profit organisations?

Discussion

The terms and conditions of trade for local providers of goods and services in their national/local markets (assuming no protective legislation) are affected by the most efficient potential providers of each product or service, whatever the sector. Larger providers are likely to have available to them resources and capabilities (financial, human, technical) of greater sophistication and usually (although not always) of greater efficiency. As long as no such alternative provider exists in a domestic market, local providers can survive and prosper. As soon as national and then international concentration and restructuring begin (whether in aircraft manufacturing, media, coal or other energy sources, utilities, insurance services, health care, clothes or children's toys) local providers have to be able to provide a similar product or service at similar cost, or offer additional added-value to justify higher local prices to the consumer. We are all familiar with such examples as local 'mom-and-pop stores' trying to stay in business against the greater product choice and cheaper prices of the local supermarket competitors by staying open for longer and longer hours. It is for this reason that their basis for competing has given rise to the label 'convenience store'.

All types of example may be cited of industry change wiping out entire national industries or of shifts to niche markets to survive. The world textile and clothing industry has changed dramatically over the last century so that the locus of efficient mass-production has moved away from Europe to Asia, as both quality and price of raw materials and labour costs have made broad market competition impossible by the developed economies. They are still viable competitors in the higher value-added segments of the market where price competition does not dominate. When a new retail concept such the US-based retail chain Toys'R'Us enters other international markets, it has the effect of transforming the sustainable bases of competition for children's toys, games and clothing in the marketplace it has just entered. If the market for illegal drugs such as heroin is an international one, while the law enforcement agencies trying to combat them are national/local only, the relative scale of resources, and the scope of information and experience brought to bear are incompatible. It is not surprising therefore that pressure builds up for the formation of cross-border links to manage international drug-fighting or international terrorism more effectively.

Many not-for-profit organisations are themselves international in scope and require international sources of funding, management and operations to be effective. Many international not-for-profit organisations, such as Greenpeace, Amnesty International and the Save the Children Fund have had to review their strategies and organisation structures to manage cross-border operations and resources.

An interesting example of the international strategies of MNCs affecting public-sector organisations is that of the BBC, the UK public-sector media organisation, paid for by public licence fee. The BBC has been affected by the advent of CNN in global low-cost news coverage, while satellite broadcasters such as BSkyB have pushed up the cost to the BBC of sporting events, films, etc.

2.1 TRADITIONAL AND MODERN FACTORS OF PRODUCTION: MOBILE V. IMMOBILE

In international trade it is important to understand why the greatest economic welfare is not necessarily served by local firms serving their local populations.

The law of *comparative costs and comparative advantage* underlies all international trade. Countries develop different costs in producing various goods because they are differentially endowed with the three traditional factors of production: land, labour and capital. Exchange between countries will generally be possible to the advantage of all and will lead to potential welfare gains. From this it follows that impediments to trade such as quotas, tariffs and other forms of protectionist policy reduce overall welfare. Of course, there may be temporary justification for them in specific circumstances (such as the protection of infant industries so that they can reach maturity and achieve international competitiveness).

Traditional economic theory of international trade based on immobile factors of production and companies without proprietary distinguishing features, culture, management styles or strategies, is now too simplistic. Porter (1990) stresses 'advanced factors' of production and includes the following issues:

- *Internationally mobile factors of production* – Labour is increasingly mobile as illustrated by periodic 'brain drains' of individuals with scarce skills to escape high taxation or low resource opportunities (such as doctors seeking better-equipped hospitals or research scientists seeking better-endowed projects) within their local labour markets. Multinational corporations employ international executives who must become equally at home in any of the three major regional trading blocs of the 'Triad' (Ohmae, 1985 – see Figure 2.1). Mobility of labour at executive level is now routine. Transparency of capital markets allows corporations and local governments to be able to shop around the world to raise capital at the best rates.

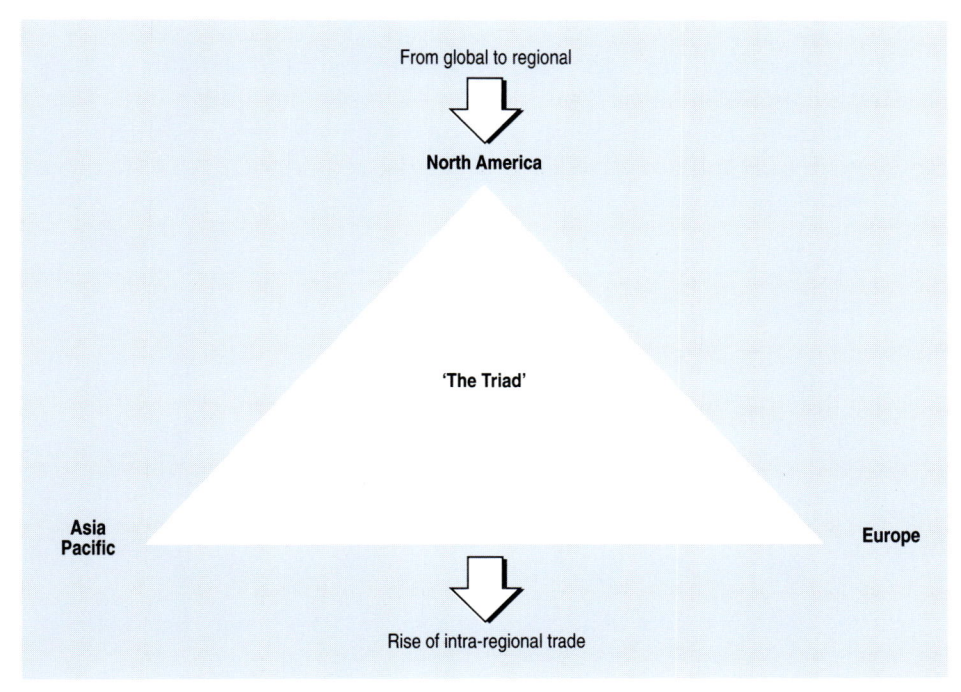

Figure 2.1 'The Triad'

- *Fast-changing technology* – A technology no sooner becomes widely adopted than another one appears on the horizon to challenge it; or, despite the use of patents and copyright, imitators catch up, reverse engineer or surpass the technology. Ever faster technological change sees products such as the Sony Walkman, the throw-away pen or the pocket calculator reduce in price over a decade or so of existence until a decision to buy one is as trivial as the decision to buy a newspaper (or they may be given away free with twenty-five litres of petrol).

- *Mobility barriers, entry or exit barriers* – Indeed any barriers that inhibit the movement of companies from one strategic group to another. Powerful mobility barriers are those that are difficult or impossible to imitate, for example know-how, strategic assets such as a gold mine (Kay 1993) or much-loved and trusted brand names. Other barriers that inhibit new entrants and that exist in most industries are those listed in Porter's (1980) 'five forces' model (Book 3) – access to distribution, learning curve, scale and scope advantages, government regulation and so forth.

Porter (1990) contends that only 'advanced factors' now lead to competitive advantage. Typical advanced factors are:

- *Human resources* – in particular managerial and technological skills.
- *Physical resources* – the quality and accessibility of a country's climate, natural resources or location.
- *Knowledge resources* – educational and research infrastructure.
- *Capital resources* – financial infrastructure such as the availability of start-up and other risk capital (in Book 10, our discussion of the development of Russia's new conglomerates showed the effects of the lack of such financial infrastructure).
- *Infrastructure* – the transportation system, the communication system, the quality of life in the country, and its health care facilities may all constitute advanced factors liable to give companies comparative advantage in some countries rather than others. Technological developments may provide the opportunity for rapid shifts in infrastructure advantage. Consider, for example, the spread of mobile telecommunications (telephones) in developing economies such as China or Eastern Europe which replace the requirement for expensive investment in cable.

Activity 2.2

You should now read the Caterpillar/Komatsu mini-case.

What sources of *comparative advantage* were available to each company?

How did they contribute to any sources of *competitive advantage*?

MINI-CASE: CATERPILLAR AND KOMATSU – COMPARATIVE ADVANTAGE AND COMPETITIVE ADVANTAGE

In strategy terms it cannot be stressed too strongly that although comparative advantage is critical to understanding and formulating international strategies, one must never lose sight of the important difference between comparative advantage and potential competitive advantage. A well-known example is that of the global competition battles for domination of the world earth-moving equipment industry between Caterpillar (USA) and its initially tiny rival Komatsu (Japan). Throughout the 1950s, '60s and '70s Komatsu skilfully built up its position against an unwary Caterpillar which then dominated over 50 per cent of world market share in that industry. By exploiting significantly lower comparative costs in raw materials – steel (30 per cent cheaper than US prices) and labour (60 per cent cheaper than US prices), it gradually undermined the classic differentiation strategy pursued by Caterpillar, i.e. premium pricing for perceived high levels of quality, reliability and service. These latter (reliability and service) rather than price, were the key purchasing criteria for customers for earth-moving equipment. In an industry where one large piece of equipment could cost $1 million it was the threat of lost 'downtime' and the possible disruption of scheduling on major construction projects that was the overwhelming anxiety for managers. No wonder customers were prepared to pay high prices for reliability and Caterpillar was very successful.

The situation gradually changed as Komatsu used a time window in the 1960s, provided for it by MITI (the Japanese Ministry for International Trade and Investment) which had refused permission for Caterpillar's entry into the Japanese domestic market and had instead licensed a Japanese joint venture between International Harvester (IH – a US rival) and Komatsu for the production of earth-moving equipment (EME) in Japan. Komatsu used this opportunity to embark on a series of dramatic quality improvement programmes. It learned rapidly from IH's technology. Eventually it bought out IH's technology licences cheaply when that company was strapped for cash in 1982. However, its greatest success lay in its programme of continuous internal improvement which turned it from a domestic supplier of such poor quality that Japanese domestic firms would not buy from it, into a rival which could match (and occasionally exceed) Caterpillar quality but at much reduced prices. This had the effect of destroying Caterpillar's sources of competitive advantage, since it could no longer justify its 20 per cent price premium on the basis of significantly higher quality. As worldwide customers gradually grew to trust Komatsu's quality, Caterpillar was required to reduce prices to match Komatsu. It was unable to do this easily or quickly, since not only had the seemingly effortless dominance of its market persisted for thirty years rendering the company relatively inefficient in its internal operations, it was also suffering from comparative cost disadvantage in labour and raw material costs compared to Komatsu. This had not mattered while Komatsu was a poor supplier of unreliable products but became very problematic indeed when Komatsu was able to match both Caterpillar's quality and product range.

Another aspect of international competition exemplified in this case was the role of government intervention. Not only did Komatsu benefit from MITI's support in blocking Caterpillar entering Japan at a critical time, but this should be contrasted with the bad luck experienced by Caterpillar in the 1980s when the then American President Ronald Reagan banned all US firms from involvement in Russia's Alaskan pipeline project – the biggest construction project in the world at that time. That intervention gave Komatsu a golden opportunity for a prestigious shop-window to demonstrate the reliability of its products under difficult geographic conditions.

Of course, the situation did not remain static and Caterpillar fought back vigorously. It had received a tremendous cultural shock in experiencing five consecutive years of losses in the late 1980s and early '90s. It embarked on a draconian series of worldwide plant evaluations, resulting in some closures. Only those evaluated as most efficient were retained and provided with investment and upgrading of technology and systems. Persistent US trade union hostility to flexible working practices blocked changes which would have matched practices from which Komatsu had been benefiting for decades. So the issue of relative labour costs for the two companies was not simply one of absolute levels of wages but also working practices affecting the relative productivity of that labour, a much more fundamental issue since absolute levels of wages tend to be only a transitional cost advantage because wages rapidly rise with economic development in any industrialising economy. (The same point may be made regarding fluctuations in exchange rate differentials.) The situation in the mid-1990s sees the two companies still dominating the world market for EME. Caterpillar has regained a proportion of its lost market share and become a much more efficient company as a result of Komatsu's efforts. Komatsu has consolidated its position as the industry's world number two, with a consistent annual world market share of over 25 per cent.

(Compiled by the author from various press articles)

Discussion

Komatsu certainly benefited from significantly lower comparative costs in raw materials – steel (30 per cent cheaper than US prices) and labour (60 per cent cheaper than US prices). However, it is important to draw lessons from this example about the difference between comparative advantage and potential competitive advantage in international strategy. Komatsu certainly had comparative cost advantages over Caterpillar in terms of steel and labour. However, these in themselves were not the source of Komatsu's changed competitive position or the source of Caterpillar's difficulties. These arose from Komatsu's strategic intent (Hamel and Prahalad, 1989) in the formulation and implementation of a viable long-term strategy to establish itself in world markets. It was this which enabled existing sources of comparative advantage to support international competitive advantage.

Activity 2.3

Can you think of any sources of comparative advantage in your economy?

How have these been utilised by any industries or organisations with which you are familiar?

Discussion

The sources of potential comparative advantage in any given economy are extremely varied. Just to give one or two examples, we might think of the advantages of climate in a given country and the specific opportunities to which that gives rise such as the wine industries historically clustered in the warmer Southern countries of Europe and their growth more recently in the equally kind 'new world' climates of Australia, New Zealand, South America and West Coast USA.

One may further consider climate and its effect on world leisure industries – whether sun-seeking or snow-seeking for skiing, and so on. Strategic assets such as the Pyramids and temples of Egypt or the canals, churches and artworks of Venice can be considered in a similar way.

However, many of these are only potential *sources of competitive advantage. War, terrorism and political instability may chase away tourists (as in Egypt, Cambodia and the former Yugoslavia), however rare or beautiful the country's resources; and Venice may yet sink under water due to poor custodianship of its assets.*

2.2 'ADVANCED' FACTORS OF PRODUCTION AND THE GROWTH OF THE MNC

The classical theory of comparative costs would suggest at first sight that local companies would be likely to have inherent advantages in their own countries compared with multinational corporations. Local companies would have lower transport costs, a better understanding of local tastes, better local networks and fewer of the overheads that come with international co-ordination. Yet goods sold through MNCs dominate most consumer goods markets. By 1970, 60 of the 100 largest economic entities in the world were MNCs, outranking the GNP of most nations. Indeed, some of these MNCs have existed longer and are more stable than many countries. Why is this?

2.2.1 MNCs: what, when and why?

MNCs are companies that have part of their activities located outside their home country and operate in international markets. In MNCs comparative costs, risk and regulatory context influence where a particular activity is carried out. However, international trade may be carried out in different ways. These are the four main types of international trade:

- exporting
- foreign direct investment (FDI) – the defining characteristic of MNCs
- licensing
- joint ventures or strategic alliances.

The theory of foreign direct investment, and of alternative organisational forms to develop business across frontiers, is set out in a simple way by Rugman *et al.* (1985, p. 130), who developed a rational decision tree for choosing between the various choices. This decision tree is given in Figure 2.2.

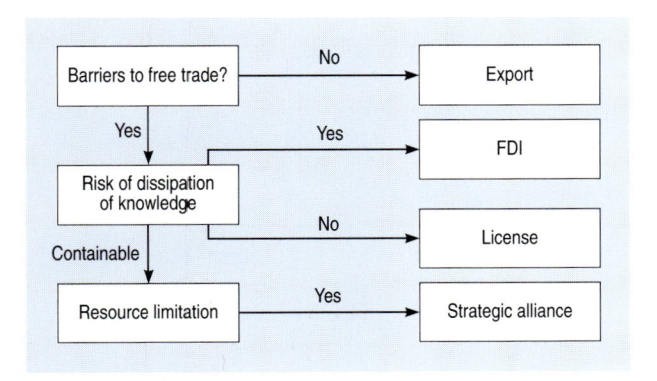

Figure 2.2 The decision tree

Thus, exporting is best in conditions where trade barriers are absent since unit costs can be reduced to a very low level from large-scale production. If trade barriers exist, however, manufacturing in foreign countries is needed to get underneath them (i.e. become an MNC). Ownership of such assets will be retained if they fear losing competitive advantage as a result of the loss of proprietary knowledge. Otherwise, a strategic alliance or joint venture may be the appropriate move, a possibility that we will return to later in this book.

We live then, not in a world of small firms producing according to their comparative advantage in factor cost; rather in a world of MNCs, single corporate entities selling on a global scale and with activities in many parts of the world.

MNCs carry out global strategies, producing standard products with minor variations and marketing them around the world, sourcing assets and activities on an optimal cost basis, and adapting where necessary to local cultures and tastes. Modern MNCs work with a shared knowledge base, a common set of values and an agreed set of priorities and measures to judge performance. Given these conditions, they may be organised into a relatively decentralised network of companies. Some different MNC approaches to international strategy will be described next.

2.3 TYPES OF INTERNATIONAL STRATEGY

It is important to recognise that there are many different ways of being international. Different approaches to international strategy suit different companies in different industries at different times. Indeed, a company may pass through many stages in its own international development. It may simultaneously pursue strategies that are widely different in the different countries in which it has a presence. These differences may weaken the company by loading it with a bloated cost structure, riddled with unnecessary duplication, inconsistent and poorly controlled quality, a confused image to its customers and poor bargaining power with its suppliers worldwide. Or, by contrast, it may be that the duplication of dedicated overhead, and the varied positioning in each of the national markets in which it operates, is precisely the reason for the success of the company in those sectors and markets in which it competes. Both these strategies are viable. What is important is that they are each viable in a different context, for specific products, in a specific market, at a specific point in time.

The four approaches to being international which firms have most frequently adopted are summarised in Table 2.1. It distinguishes between multinational, global, international and transnational firms. Multinationals treat each country market as independent and best serviced by a

Table 2.1 Four approaches to being international

Organisational Characteristics	Multinational	Global	International	Transnational
Configuration of assets and capabilities	Decentralised and nationally self-sufficient	Centralised and scaled globally	Sources of core abilities centralised; others decentralised	Dispersed, interdependent, and specialised
Role of overseas operations	Sensing and exploiting local opportunities	Implementing parent-company strategies	Adapting and exploiting parent-company's abilities	Differentiated contributions by national units to integrated worldwide operations
Development and diffusion of knowledge	Knowledge developed and retained within each unit	Knowledge developed and retained at centre	Knowledge developed at centre and transferred to overseas units	Knowledge developed jointly and shared worldwide

Source: Bartlett and Ghoshal (1989)

subsidiary dedicated to meet its local needs and conditions. Global firms emphasise worldwide strategies to benefit from operational scale. They are heavily centralised, with direction and control emanating mainly from central headquarters. International firms use the centre to transfer and share knowledge around the various business units to allow the whole organisation to benefit from experience gained in any one part.

There is a rich and confusing terminology in international strategy. What Bartlett and Ghoshal (1989) in Table 2.1 call the 'multinational', Porter (1986) calls the 'multidomestic' corporation. It means an organisation which competes internationally by building strong local presence through sensitivity and responsiveness to national differences (as Philips did in the mini-case which follows in Section 3.1). 'Global' organisations build cost advantage through integration of centralised scale operations. 'International' organisations exploit parent-company knowledge and capabilities through worldwide diffusion and adaptation. 'Transnationals' learn from specialised, dispersed units, as well as from the centre. We will be using these terms and discussing the suitability of the international strategies and structures that they represent throughout the rest of this book. Before exploring these different approaches in more detail in Section 4, we need a clearer perspective on the objectives of international strategy.

2.4 THE GREAT GAME: THE ROLE OF GOVERNMENTS AND THE LIMITS TO REGULATION

International strategy is not a zero-sum game, unlike domestic market strategy. The mere fact that low labour-cost economies do not remain cheap permanently makes the point that economic growth through trade creates substantial changes over time in the standard of living within those countries.

Japan, Malaysia, Singapore and South Korea are all examples of low labour-cost economies which have become developed and hence, expensive, as general expectations of standards of living have risen, leading to displacement of labour-intensive jobs elsewhere (e.g. to Vietnam and China). Governments have to cope with the internal political tensions this creates as MNCs shift production elsewhere. Only higher value-added jobs are likely to be retained long-term within developed economies. In international strategy terms it is cheaper for Germany's BMW and Mercedes-Benz car companies to build new plants in the USA than in Germany, or to invest in Poland or the Czech Republic; if they do not do so, the comparative disadvantage of their high-cost German plants will render their necessary price differential unsustainable against (perceived) equally good Japanese models such as the Toyota 'Lexus'. Governments (national or regional) meanwhile must provide public welfare (e.g. through education) and protection (e.g. labour law, consumer protection, pollution policy). Some of the ethical issues raised by such MNC production-shifting were addressed in Book 9. You may also wish to remind yourself of the conclusions of Grindley in the Course Reader (Chapter 8) that the role of regulatory authority is 'to provide the conditions for the market to work and if necessary correct potential excesses', but not to act as a backdoor way of supporting national industries or firms, or of implementing national or international industrial policies. Since these approaches most often result in less robust industries or firms, in the longer term there is no benefit to industries, firms or consumers.

Activity 2.4

Consider the arguments so far in Section 2.4. In spite of the issue of long-term comparative disadvantage, can you think of any examples of the benefits arising from government intervention in industrial or competition policy?

Discussion

An obvious example that we have already encountered in this book is in the Caterpillar/Komatsu mini-case where the intervention of Japan's MITI provided a very weak Komatsu with an invaluable period of protection from foreign competitor entry into its domestic market until it was strong enough to compete itself. It must be stressed, however, that greatest benefit from protection is gained for short-term specific objectives rather than long-term general ones.

2.4.1 The great game: governments and MNCs

At this point, let us make some simple statements about international strategy and the role of MNCs. They are complex organisations: difficult to manage, often castigated in the press and public opinion; frequently caught out degenerating into bloated and dysfunctional bureaucracies, inflexible and unresponsive or slow to change. What then is the point of them?

The main strategic benefit in being an MNC is that it gives flexibility and options. In international competition, options allow you to choose between ways of doing things. For domestic firms, their domestic market is 100 per cent of their potential market. Much domestic market strategy is defensive, trying to protect existing positions while more and more volume of world trade is cross-border. MNCs have available to them a wider range of strategies simply by being international and operating across borders.

Governments and supra-national organisations erect regulatory, institutional and tariff barriers to trade, while MNCs attempt to configure their international operations to exploit those barriers which favour them (such as international agreements about routes and prices in the airline industry) and avoid those that do not. Such trade barriers include:

- high tariffs
- import quota systems
- refusal to sanction licences
- nationalistic purchasing and ownership policies
- centralised 'command' economies
- excessively chauvinistic domestic demand.

Governments tax immobile assets and nationally based consumption and try to set corporation taxes at levels which will provide them with useful sources of tax revenue to spend on services without forcing the corporations to shift their investments in jobs, buildings, research or technology elsewhere. It is for this reason that governments try to attract quality inward investment by MNCs into their countries by offering capital grants, regional grants (especially in employment 'black spots'), tax-free zones, and so on.

Small is not beautiful in terms of international competition. Large organisations have available to them an array of advantages. Kogut (1985) summarises these as follows:

- production shifting
- tax minimisation
- financial markets
- information arbitrage
- global co-ordination
- reducing political risk.

Activity 2.5

Can you think what any of these might mean in international strategy terms?

Have any of these factors been utilised by any organisations with which you are familiar?

Discussion

An attempt at 'production shifting' was the announcement by Ford of Europe in January 1997 that it intended shifting European car production from one of its British factories to its factories in Spain and Germany. The company argued that it needed to rationalise production of certain models at its most efficient plants, having lost $472 million in Europe in just one quarter of 1996 and with fierce price-cutting by all car manufacturers alongside general industry overcapacity. Employees and trade unions were outraged. A similar outcry followed the announcement by French car-maker Renault of the closure of its factory in Belgium in March 1997. In the end, Ford agreed to keep their threatened UK factory open, but reduced in size.

This example may also contain an instance of 'tax minimisation' since the Ford UK workers claimed that they were being chosen for closure instead of their counterparts in Spain or Germany because of the lower redundancy payments which Ford would incur in the UK. In more general tax terms, MNCs are able to minimise their tax burden by moving their internal and external transactions to the most advantageous national tax location.

Governments often create financial markets and financial arbitrage opportunities for MNCs through their policies to attract inward investment (such as export credits and guaranteed loans). MNCs can also create innovative financial products to benefit from financial flexibility. In addition, it is perhaps an obvious point to make but an important one that large organisations tend to have better credit ratings than smaller organisations and therefore benefit from cheaper cost of capital. MNCs also organise themselves to benefit from information arbitrage including such things as transfer of knowledge about products and markets and the transfer of product or process developments from one location to another.

These all represent what Kogut (1985) calls 'arbitrage opportunities', where the MNC seeks to benefit from the exploitation of differences in the price of an asset, a product or an activity between different marketplaces. 'Global co-ordination' is a 'leverage opportunity', by which he means 'the creation of market or bargaining power because of the global position of the firm' such as price co-ordination to consolidate or build market position. Leverage opportunities capture the bargaining power arising from having internationally dispersed operations. Since MNCs can usually decide where they carry out particular parts of their operations, the management of political risk is both a problem and an opportunity. Judgements about the levels of risk and reward attached to each potential investment opportunity must be evaluated. For example relatively high political risk of investments in China or South Africa must be weighed against the attractions of each of those markets in terms of overall size and long-term development potential. You may find it useful to look at de la Torre and Neckar's (1988) matrix of types of exposure to political risk shown in Figure 2.3.

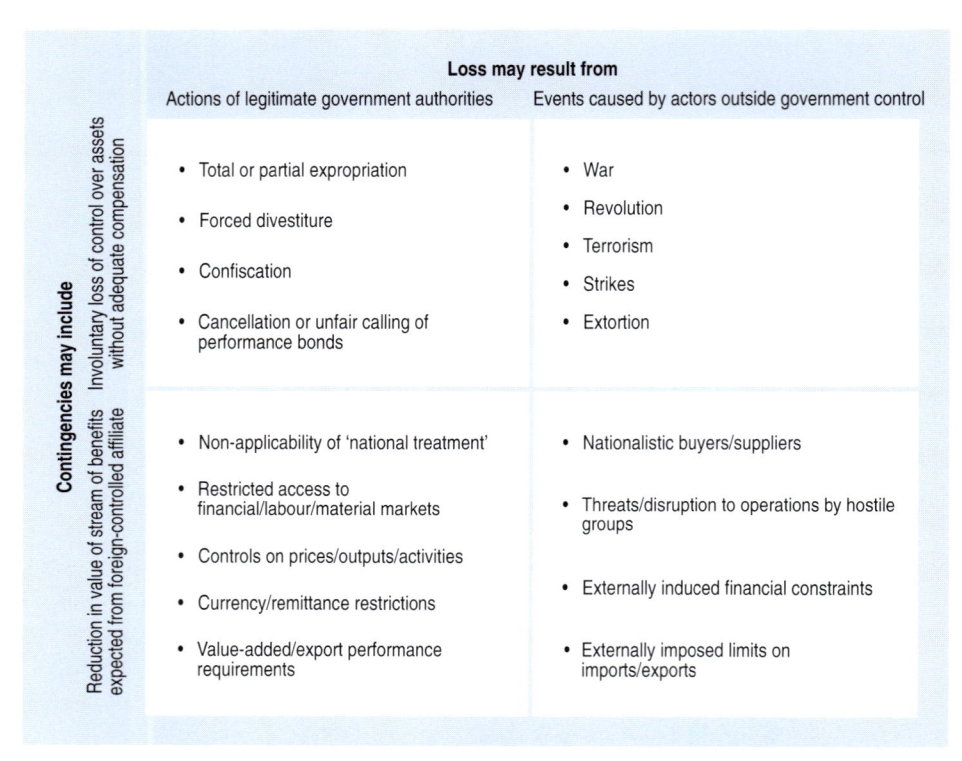

	Loss may result from	
	Actions of legitimate government authorities	Events caused by actors outside government control
Contingencies may include — Involuntary loss of control over assets without adequate compensation	• Total or partial expropriation • Forced divestiture • Confiscation • Cancellation or unfair calling of performance bonds	• War • Revolution • Terrorism • Strikes • Extortion
Reduction in value of stream of benefits expected from foreign-controlled affiliate	• Non-applicability of 'national treatment' • Restricted access to financial/labour/material markets • Controls on prices/outputs/activities • Currency/remittance restrictions • Value-added/export performance requirements	• Nationalistic buyers/suppliers • Threats/disruption to operations by hostile groups • Externally induced financial constraints • Externally imposed limits on imports/exports

Figure 2.3   Exposure to political risks (de la Torre and Neckar, 1988)

2.4.2 Summary

In Section 2.4 we have been developing a particular perspective about the means and ends of international strategy. It is about positioning across the globe. What drives international strategy is the availability of a broader set of strategic options and choices. The key management issue is the organisational structure and capabilities with which to realise them.

3 Comparative advantage and international competitive advantage

You should now read the Set Book Chapter 14, pp. 331–50.

We will now discuss a number of the issues that Grant raises about the international competitive environment and the international location of production. We are particularly concerned with the relationship between countries and organisations:

> Global strategies rest on the interplay of the competitive advantage of firms and the comparative advantage of countries.
>
> (Kogut, 1985)

3.1 World trade and international competitive advantage

We can discuss world trade and international competition in terms of supply and demand. Grant sees the two main levers of internationalisation as growth in world trade and FDI. He sees the two main drivers as 'the desire to exploit market opportunities in other countries' (i.e. demand), and 'to exploit production opportunities by establishing production activities wherever they can be conducted most efficiently' (i.e. supply). From this has come 'globalisation of business', affecting sources of international advantage and the design of international strategies. He points out that lower market shares within national markets are now combined with higher market-share rivalry across borders, fuelled by convergence of consumer preferences (demand) and worldwide sourcing (supply): 'the principal [global] players have increasingly become the same'; 'for many industries, it is clear that national markets are simply segments within a broader global market'.

3.2 Comparative advantage revisited: the Porter 'diamond'

We shall now return to comparative advantage, discussed in Section 2.1. Having read Grant's discussion of Porter's (1990) *Competitive Advantage of Nations*, you should be clear that what Porter is emphasising is the place of comparative advantage in international competitive advantage. Without going through the definitions once again, we can instead develop our understanding of Porter's national 'diamond' (see Figure 3.1) and his emphasis on the importance of national 'clusters' of resources and capabilities, by returning to the Benetton mini-case in Book 4.

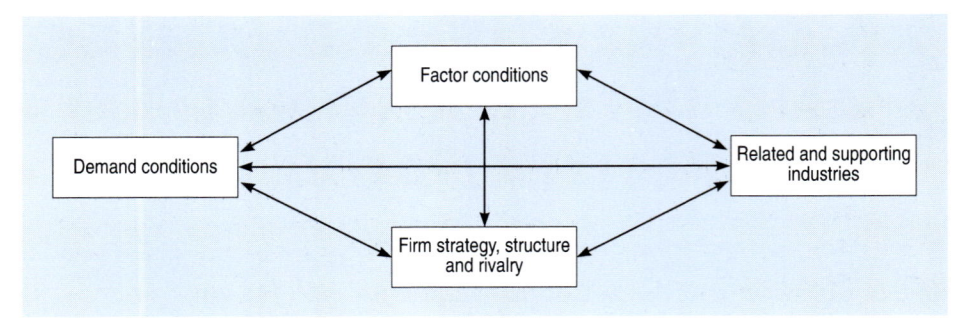

Figure 3.1 The Porter 'diamond'

Activity 3.1

Re-read the Benetton mini-case in Book 4 (pages 8–11) and think about Benetton's sources of competitive advantage. Consider whether it made any difference to those sources of advantage that Benetton was an Italian company.

Discussion

Let us analyse Benetton's position by applying the four elements in Porter's 'diamond' to it:

Factor conditions – *The textile industry is an historic industry in Italy with hundreds of years of specialised skill and experience to draw on. So Benetton was able to use not just cheap labour in a poor part of Italy, but highly skilled and experienced cheap labour.*

Demand conditions – *The Italians as a nation are among the most sophisticated customers in the world for fashion. As such they provide a demanding and critical marketplace for Benetton's designs. If you can survive as a fashion retailer in Italy, you are likely to have a product that will survive other international markets.*

Related and supporting industries – *Italy has a national 'cluster' of very strong industries both in the fashion industry itself, with its numerous designer labels, fashion houses and high priests of the Milan fashion shows, but also in many related industries such as leather goods (shoes, handbags, belts, luggage), furniture and design. All these industries share common factors such as high design skills and knowledge of materials.*

Firm strategy, structure and rivalry – *Items for consideration in this part of the 'diamond' are the 'five forces' industry analysis issues you were introduced to in Book 3. Here, the point Porter wishes to make is that firms located within very competitive industries with high levels of national rivalry are the ones most likely to do well in international markets. Those with few or no national rivals are unlikely to be as efficient or as responsive to customer requirements. They may nevertheless survive or prosper within a relatively protected domestic marketplace, but are unlikely to perform strongly internationally. Benetton is located in an overcrowded domestic fashion market, from whose competitive rigours it will benefit.*

Porter is thus convinced that 'home-base' and domestic industry conditions are critical to international success. In Box 3.1 this view is contrasted with that of Ohmae, who believes that national roots must be left behind to be internationally successful.

BOX 3.1 'PORTER V. OHMAE'

In today's borderless world, nations have become less important to companies, whether as home bases or sources of identity. Wrong, says Michael Porter. Right, says Kenichi Ohmae. [...]

The battleground between Messrs Porter and Ohmae is that modish entity the global corporation. Cheap computing and communications, the tumbling of barriers against foreign investment and capital-raising, the spread of tastes, fashions and standards across frontiers, all these have pushed more and more firms to compete on a world market rather than on national ones. The old 1960s model of the multinational, with a dominant parent company and an array of stand-alone clones in each overseas market, has been superseded by one in which firms locate production wherever the costs are lowest and organise on a more equal, global scale. Increasingly [...] companies are becoming stateless world citizens independent of their original nationalities.

Bunk, thinks Mr Porter, a professor at Harvard Business School. He accepts that markets and businesses are becoming more global, and welcomes the fact as it introduces greater competition in each country. But he thinks that this trend, far from making nations less important, instead makes them more so. His research, covering ten countries and more than 100 industries, suggests that the conditions at a company's home base are crucial to its competitiveness abroad. The homogenising force of a shrinking world, with computer technology available to all, makes it ever more important for firms to remain different from their rivals. Such differences, especially in innovative vitality, appear to be established at home.

Not terribly surprisingly, Mr Porter notes that some countries are wealthier than others and that some industries take successful root in some places and some in others. These clusters of excellence could equally well be defined by a city, a region or a continent, but he thinks the nation remains the most important area: demand conditions are affected by macroeconomic policy; the dynamism of competition by antitrust and trade policy; the level and type of skills by the education system; and attitudes of managers, workers and customers by a national culture.

Mr Ohmae, who runs McKinsey's Japanese operations, would not disagree so far. Though he is an evangelist for a borderless world economy and market, he would accept that companies emerge from national origins that establish their competitiveness. He also thinks governments build the biggest obstacles to a prosperous borderless world through protectionism and other measures to frustrate consumers' choices. But the difference between the gurus lies in global strategy: what a company should do to transform itself into a successful global firm and to stay there. Mr Ohmae argues that it should shake off its origins; Mr Porter thinks it must preserve them, virtually at all costs.

The greatest sin for a global company, according to Mr Ohmae, is nearsightedness. Multinational firms tend to be dominated by their parent headquarters, whose view is in turn dominated by its domestic customers. Markets these days are being driven by the needs and desires of customers worldwide, and the manager must act as if he is equidistant from those customers wherever they may be.

This does not mean that products should become standardised as a world beer or a world car. Far from it: in each main market the firm must seek to act as an insider, tailoring products to local customers. But to do that requires freedom from the leaden, standardising force of headquarters. Ideally the centre should be decomposed into several regional headquarters with control of different functions (production, marketing etc.) dispersed to differing extents and different locations. And this is not merely the strategy of a firm choosing to become global: increasingly, firms have no choice but do so or die. The global market will come to them if they do not go to it.

Only up to a point, thinks Mr Porter. To him, a global strategy merely supplements the competitive advantage created at home base; it is the icing not the cake. National virtues create the opportunity to cross borders. If he is right, it is crucial that companies hang on to those virtues when they expand abroad; otherwise they will become global dodos. Firms, in other words, cannot merely take their 'management system' or their technology and apply it wherever they like. Businesses are dynamic creatures that need constantly to be reinvigorated. Going global can help to sustain and upgrade competitiveness but Mr Porter thinks the elixir of youth still comes from home.

Who is right? Mr Ohmae's view is essentially futurology, an idea of how things should and perhaps will be, as global forces gather strength. [...]

Firms like IBM, Sony or Nestlé have their tentacles spread throughout the world and gain plenty from such non-domestic suckers, but the firms' character and competitiveness remains American, Japanese and Swiss. World citizenship remains science fiction. Unless the world is about to change, the verdict goes to Porter, on points.

Source: The Economist, *4 August 1990*

Reflection

Having read the management 'guru' debate between Porter and Ohmae about the respective importance of 'home-base' or 'borderless' organisations in international strategy, who do you agree with and why?

Ohmae (1985, 1989) sees global companies operating as what he calls 'true insiders', honorary citizens perceived as direct investors in each 'home' market in which they operate. Porter sees the continuous enhancements of comparative factor endowments as the basis of distinctive capabilities and the source of dynamic (i.e. sustainable) long-term advantage.

The Philips/Matsushita mini-case which follows allows us to look at these issues in greater depth.

MINI-CASE: THE COMPETITIVE ADVANTAGE OF NATIONS – THE PHILIPS GROUP OF HOLLAND VERSUS MATSUSHITA (MEI) OF JAPAN

Philips is Holland's premier industrial company and the largest consumer electronics company in Europe. It is in fact the last remaining significant European competitor in an industry which has relentlessly been overwhelmed and dominated by large Japanese MNCs such as Sony Corporation, Hitachi, Sharp Electronics and Matsushita Electric (MEI) the largest of them all. Philips celebrated its centenary in 1991. However, what should have been a cause for celebration was overshadowed by problems for the company and its future.

Problems at Philips

Early in May 1990, Dr Wisse Dekker, chairman of Philips's supervisory board, suddenly cut short a visit to America to fly back to Philips's home town of Eindhoven for an emergency meeting. Philips faced a crisis unprecedented for a major industrial company with some of the best known and most widely used brands in the world. Few European households were without a Philips television, shaver, light bulb or audio equipment. The company was one of the bastions of European business with annual sales of almost £19 billion. However, by 1990 it had sunk to an unprecedented low. Profits in the first three months of 1990 were down to Fl 6 million (£1.9 million) from Fl 223 million (almost £75 million) in the same quarter a year before. Worse still, only three weeks earlier, Cornelius van der Klugt, Philips president, had told shareholders that Philips was on track to achieve its target earnings for 1990. At a very tense press conference held on 15 May Dekker appeared alone to apologise for this financial and ethical failure. Van der Klugt made a rapid and ignominious departure. By the end of 1990, Philips had a net loss of Fl 4.53 billion – the biggest loss in Dutch corporate history.

Causes of Philips's Decline

Throughout the 1980s, Philips was under fierce assault from Japanese and Korean competitors and was struggling to restructure itself in order to meet the competitive threat. When van der Klugt became president in 1987 his brief was to reshape its organisation structure, management procedures, style and culture. Philips's main strength was technical innovation. Its R&D and new product development were respected worldwide. Unfortunately, it was less effective at ensuring it achieved the market share and financial return from its innovative product stream since Philips's main weakness was high costs and lack of sufficient central financial and managerial control. To improve this Philips needed to move from being a dispersed international corporation to a centralised global one.

Philips's problems thus had two main sources: *comparative disadvantage* arising from its high domestic labour market costs relative to those of its Japanese competitors; and an unwieldy decentralised, international organisation structure, based on a matrix system of nine product groups and 60 countries ('national organisations') each with separate national managerial autonomy. Friction between the centre (Eindhoven) and periphery (the autonomous national subsidiaries) was frequent, which helped to explain the gap between Philips's superb product innovation and poor marketing. An early example of this was the rejection (in the 1970s) by Philips's North American organisation of its own V-2000 videocassette format, in favour of the VHS format from Japanese rival Matsushita. That destroyed any chance of establishing the Philips video format in the huge American market. Matsushita's VHS format became the industry standard (also beating off Sony's Betamax format).

Despite a major reorganisation into four international product divisions (consumer electronics, lighting, professional products and components), and a new group management committee, organisational effectiveness seemed no nearer. The aim of the reorganisation was to 'tilt the matrix' away from a focus on national geographic markets and towards international co-ordination. But the reorganisation never really tackled Philips's heavy commitment to jobs and payroll in high labour-cost Holland. By the end of the 1980s only 10 per cent of production was in the Far East with 65 per cent still in Europe. Philips remained Holland's largest employer, with 65,000 Dutch employees when van der Klugt departed in 1990. In addition, Philips's decentralised decision-making procedures gave country subsidiaries and country general managers great autonomy in running their national organisations. In some respects perhaps Philips was a truly 'borderless' multinational in Ohmae's sense, since it was regarded as a 'local' firm wherever it was located. It thus had great advantages in terms of close local market knowledge.

The changing competitive map

As usual, what had been a strength under one set of industry conditions became a weakness when those industry conditions changed (see Book 3). The decentralised approach became a liability when Japanese competitors began to enter the European market with a much tighter cost-base and centralised control systems, R&D, marketing and distribution and very high quality products. What became evident was that consumer electronics was a global industry in which it was possible to develop and market highly standardised products and components across world markets. Philips was organised with a higher cost-base which only made sense if those costs were the necessary costs of local adaptation of products which had to be tailored to suit the needs of different local marketplaces. Local adaptation of products such as televisions and stereo systems is, however, minimal. They can be developed as broadly homogeneous for all world markets. Philips was bearing local costs in a global market. In three years between 1987–90, Philips closed or merged 75 of its 346 plants spread over 50 countries. It also shed over 38,000 employees worldwide. However, that still left it with too many factories, over half of them in Europe where labour costs were high, compared to the lower production and labour costs of its main (Asian) rivals. It also had permanent problems with exchange rates since it had such a small percentage of sales (6 per cent) in its domestic currency. A new chairman (Jan Timmer) was appointed in July 1990 as a change agent to revitalise and centralise Philips's product policy and planning process.

Matsushita's global strategy

Matsushita was founded with $100 in a workshop in his own home in 1918 by a young entrepreneur (Konosuke Matsushita). By 1986 its overseas sales revenues were $15.6 billion. It was run as a highly centralised company with no local autonomy. Its strategy was low-cost, but with a steady stream of new products to attract and keep market share. Its Japanese nickname was 'maneshita' – loosely translated as 'copycat'. Unlike Philips it regarded itself as a technology 'follower' rather than a technology leader or innovator. (Matsushita thus illustrates an 'imitative innovation' strategy described in Book 6, Section 3.5.) It has some of the world's most powerful consumer electronics brands including Panasonic, Technics and JVC. It set very tight financial targets monitored from the centre. In its international expansion, key positions were always given to internal Japanese expatriates who were regarded as custodians of Matsushita's very strong culture and 'spiritual precepts' of management. Its founder had declared himself as setting the terms of a strategy for 250 years, for which each managerial generation would be responsible for 25 years, starting with himself.

In contrast to Philips, Matsushita operated a policy of 'hungry divisions': one product, one division. This was a deliberate approach aimed at avoiding any tendency to organisational inertia arising from successful products and revenues. The problems Matsushita faced in the late 1980s were different from those of Philips. They were problems arising from successful centralisation. It wanted to become less of a centralised hub controlled from

Japan and more 'truly international'. The driving force for this was that the product credited with providing the bulk of Matsushita's revenues – the VCR – was entering its mature phase. Over the seven-year period from 1977 to 1984, in response to rapid increases in demand, Matsushita had shown it had excellent responsive capabilities in manufacturing and marketing. It famously multiplied production of the successful VCR product line by 33 times capacity. This enabled it to drop the price by one-third over the same period. By 1984 the VCR was generating 45 per cent of worldwide revenues. It was not obvious where a replacement product of similar magnitude could come from.

Matsushita's localisation ('glocal') strategy

All the signs were that the next generation of consumer electronics products would be likely to spring from technology convergence, perhaps in multimedia, such as those seen in 'The Information Superhighway' video accompanying Book 10. Such a development would require a different organisational structure from the global hub for controlling standardised global production and distribution. Matsushita also faced macro-economic pressures including: rising protectionist sentiment in some of its main markets; a high yen making its products more expensive; a dearth of qualified software engineers in its domestic market; a need to understand technical capabilities abroad and share learning back home internally.

So, just at the time that Philips was struggling to exert stronger central control, Matsushita was pursuing more sensitivity and autonomy in local markets. From 1986 it allowed greater local autonomy to local divisions in hiring and promoting more local personnel; local sourcing and purchasing; modified designs for local markets; adapted corporate processes and technologies; incorporated local components; became more 'localised'. In so doing it risked dilution of its strong internal culture and values; lower volume outputs and therefore reduced manufacturing economies of scale; dilution of processes which provided consistency of quality, product and process. In 1990, in its pursuit of synergies from the convergence of 'hardware' (TVs, videos, stereos) and 'software' (the programming contents – TV programmes, films, records) Matsushita bought MCA/Universal film studios in Hollywood for $6.1 billion. It was subsequently divested in 1995.

Source: compiled by the author from Sunday Times, *20 May 1990;* The Economist, *27 July 1991; various press articles*

Activity 3.2

Having read the mini-case on Philips and Matsushita, how far would you say that the problems each faces result from comparative advantage or from the strategies and structures of the firms themselves?

Does Porter's 'diamond' framework help you to organise your answer?

Discussion

Philips and Matsushita are both international competitors in the consumer electronics industry. Each faces entirely different conditions in their 'home-base'. On balance, Matsushita's national 'cluster' is a far more advantageous one than that of Philips. Matsushita has a huge domestic market of sophisticated, discerning consumers; demand conditions are excellent. Factor conditions are fairly neutral except for a recent shortage of engineers. This may be contrasted with Philips's negative factor conditions – expensive local labour and a tiny domestic market. Local competitive rivalry and supporting industry clusters once again favour the Japanese corporation rather than the Dutch one. Matsushita is surrounded by equally powerful rivals in its domestic market in all the sectors in which it competes, whereas Philips dominates its domestic economy and bears a high degree of social cost within it. However, despite Philips's sources of comparative disadvantage, its own strategy and structure have responded far too slowly to competitive pressures.

3.3 CONFIGURATION OF THE INTERNATIONAL VALUE CHAIN

In international strategy, 'configuration' is a term which refers to where value chain activities are performed. Grant calls this issue 'the international location of production'. Where do we do what we do and why? The location of activities in an international value chain is one of the most important concepts in international strategy, because it is how MNCs benefit from the geographic dispersion of their activities. It is the means by which organisations implement their mix of Kogut's arbitrage and leverage opportunities (Section 2.4.1). All organisations have a wide choice of possible configurations of their activities. Organisations that operate across borders should use their choice of configuration as a source of advantage.

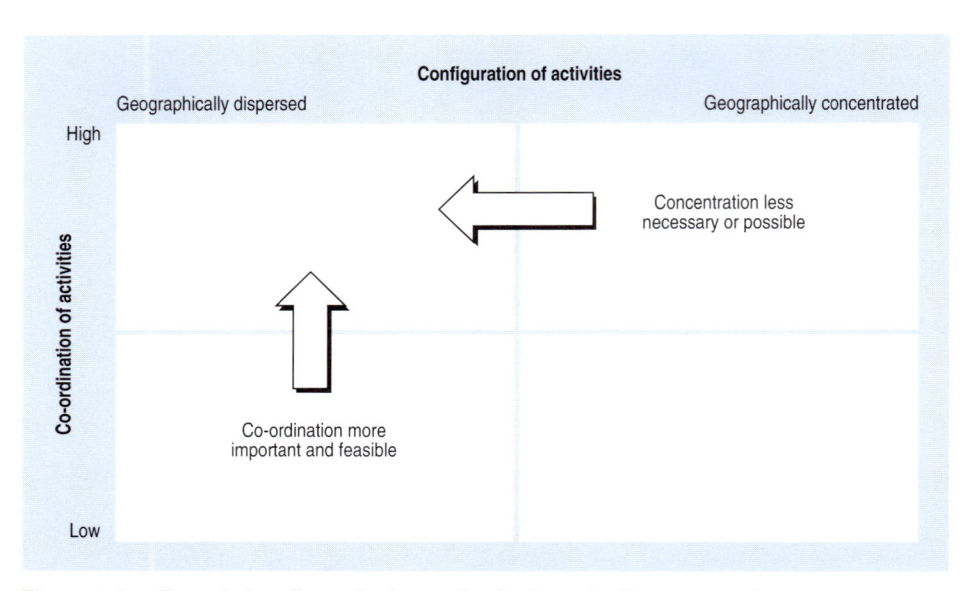

Figure 3.2   Porter's 'configuration/co-ordination' matrix (Porter, 1986)

Figure 3.2 shows Porter's view of the future: the relationship between configuration (where value chain activities are performed) and co-ordination of the organisation's value chain configuration (how it is managed). Whatever configuration is adopted, a different set of co-ordination issues is generated. For example, if an organisation decides to concentrate its R&D in one location worldwide (as Toyota did) then the co-ordination issues will be those of ensuring that the R&D function is in touch with local market intelligence and with other functions such as production and sales. If the same R&D function were configured differently so that now it is decentralised and dispersed into 25 locations around the world, it would be likely to be in touch with local market needs and wants, but the co-ordination issue would now be of the R&D function itself. The organisation would need to ensure that the 25 R&D units were in communication with each other to share developments, select and co-ordinate project priorities to avoid duplication and so on. Lack of effective co-ordination can be highly embarrassing as well as inefficient. A well-known international consulting firm with offices in 146 countries around the world discovered that one of its most valued clients had received two conflicting bids for a new contract – both of them from different national offices of their own international organisation, and to make matters worse they were priced quite differently. They were under-bidding themselves for the same project.

Activity 3.3

Consider once again the mini-case on Philips and Matsushita.

Where would you place each company on Figure 3.2, Porter's 'configuration/co-ordination' matrix?

What, if anything, does it tell you about them?

Discussion

At the time of the mini-case, Philips was probably bottom left and Matsushita top right. One of Philips's biggest problems was its 'low co-ordination of activities'. If it stays with a dispersed configuration it urgently needs to move to top left, which is where Matsushita is trying to move with its 'localisation' strategy. That seems to suggest a possible consensus on the most appropriate organisational configuration to meet the future direction of the consumer electronics industry.

For a different example of an international 'configuration' issue, consider the changing pattern of international logistics and the significance of these changes for the strategies and structures of international firms. Christopher and Braithwaite (1994) have looked at the implications of global convergence for managing the global supply chain. They conclude that the high level of co-ordination required to manage complex global supply chains may result in higher costs. Such additional costs must be weighed against the cost savings resulting from standardised global production, as firms plan and implement their international strategies.

Figure 3.3 overleaf shows three of the most common approaches to the international value chain. A is seeking production scale efficiencies. B is more complex and is seeking efficiency in each separate link in the chain. C is approaching optimal efficiency not just by looking at each separate link in the activity chain (as does B), but also at the relationships across all the activities.

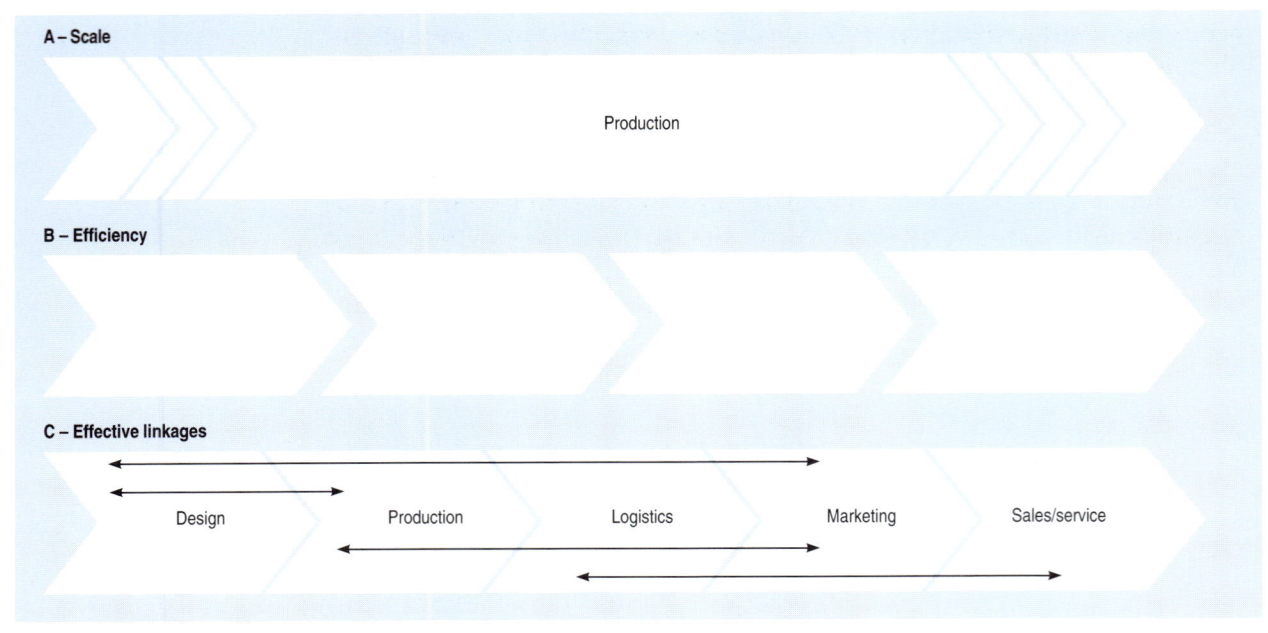

Figure 3.3 Three approaches to the international value chain

A – Scale

Production

B – Efficiency

C – Effective linkages

Design | Production | Logistics | Marketing | Sales/service

3.4 MEANS AND ENDS: GHOSHAL'S 'ORGANISING FRAMEWORK'

While Porter's 'diamond' helps explain how national conditions (factor endowments) can affect the international competitiveness of firms, Ghoshal's (1987) 'organising framework' gives specific guidance on the relevance of global strategy for individual organisations. In an important article Ghoshal provides a synthesis of the concepts and literature in the field of global strategy. By so doing he helps us to think about the question: what is the point of having a global strategy? His answers to that question are contained in Table 3.1. Practising managers should find this framework helpful because it shows you what questions to ask about global strategy.

Table 3.1 Ghoshal's 'organising framework'

Strategic objectives	Sources of competitive advantage		
	National differences	Scale economies	Scope economies
Achieving efficiency in current operations	Benefiting from differences in factor costs (e.g. wages and cost of capital)	Expanding and exploiting potential scale economies in each activity	Sharing of investments and costs across products, markets and businesses
Managing risks	Managing different kinds of risk arising from market or policy-induced changes in comparative advantages of different countries	Balancing scale with strategic and operational flexibility	Portfolio diversification of risks and creation of options and side-bets
Innovation, learning and adaptation	Learning from societal differences in organisational and managerial processes and systems	Benefiting from experience (cost reduction and innovation)	Shared learning across organisational components in different products, markets or businesses

Ghoshal is saying that the point of having a global strategy is contained in the three strategic objectives (vertical axis), while the means for achieving those objectives are the three sources of advantage (horizontal axis). National differences, and scale and scope economies are the means by which the better management of risk, operational efficiency and innovation may be achieved. His synthesis is elegant, simple and very powerful.

Activity 3.4

Can you think of actual examples for any of Ghoshal's nine categories in his 3 × 3 matrix, either from your own experience, or from the mini-cases so far in this book?

For example, for the top-left box you would be trying to think of an organisation using national differences to help improve operational efficiency. For this category Table 3.1 gives examples of differences in factor costs such as wages or cost of capital. For the middle-left box you might think of changes in import quotas or tariffs. For the bottom-left box your organisation could be learning about 'just-in-time' or 'lean manufacturing' processes from having some part of your operations located in Japan. If you cannot think of your own examples then draw on the mini-cases in this book (Caterpillar/Komatsu and Philips/Matsushita).

Discussion

Let us work along the top line to suggest examples for the top three boxes taken from our earlier discussion. Komatsu and Matsushita both benefited from lower labour costs (top left). Komatsu also benefited from (bottom right) shared learning about its production processes to achieve high quality products across its whole product range. Matsushita clearly benefited from manufacturing scale economies (middle top) – remember the 33 times manufacturing output increase of VCRs over seven years. Caterpillar was looking for improvement here from its programme of plant closures. Philips did not benefit from scale economies as much as its rival Matsushita because of its dispersed operations. In fact, unlike its more profitable rivals, Philips did not actually have a global strategy; it had a multidomestic one in a global industry, which largely accounted for its poor performance in its sector. None of them was doing particularly well for scope economies (top right). However, future organisational changes planned would have helped achieve these better.

We will return frequently to the issues summarised in Ghoshal's framework in Table 3.1 as we look in more detail at global and other international strategies in Section 4. However, you may have found it difficult to think of examples of scope economies and may wish to be reminded about them at this stage (you could refer back to Book 4). Read Box 3.2 (overleaf), a brief newspaper account of the acquisition by Gillette in 1996 of the battery manufacturer Duracell for $7 billion.

BOX 3.2 'GILLETTE SNAPS UP DURACELL'

'The $7 billion deal should lead to bigger battery sales through Gillette's huge network.'

In a bold move to sustain its remarkable growth of recent years, Gillette is paying $7 billion for Duracell, the world's top alkaline battery maker.

Analysts are kicking themselves for failing to predict the deal, which they say is 'a perfect fit' and should result in higher Duracell earnings as Gillette starts selling batteries through its global distribution network – which includes, says Al Zeien, its chairman, 'every kiosk up the Amazon river'. [...]

The all-share deal, which is subject to investor approval, will leave Kohlberg Kravis Roberts as Gillette's second-largest shareholder (with 6.8%) after Warren Buffett's Berkshire Hathaway (with 9%).

The move marks the latest step in Gillette's diversification from razors and blades. It is already the world's top dental-care products producer, having bought Oral-B in 1984, and the largest writing products supplier, owning Parker Pen (acquired in 1993), Waterman and Papermate. It is also a big toiletries supplier and owns Braun, a leading manufacturer of coffee makers, shavers and other small appliances.

Gillette's sales rose 12% last year to $6.8 billion, and net income was up 18% to $823.5 million. Double-digit growth has made it a stellar Wall Street performer. In the last five years its market value has almost quintupled, from $6.1 billion at the end of 1990 to $30 billion.

It is a big turnround for a group that faced four hostile bids in the 1980s, and was rescued from the clutches of Ron Perelman by Buffett. Zeien was propelled into the top job in 1991 when his predecessor, Colman Mockler, worn out by his defending the company, died at his desk of a heart attack.

Mockler began the new product push and introduced the successful Sensor razor in 1989. Zeien [...] has continued this drive, spending 50% of operating profits on research and development, capital spending and advertising, and launching more than 20 new products a year.

He has also expanded overseas and 70% of sales now come from outside the US; Gillette has four joint ventures in China and two in Russia (one with the Sputnik razor company). New markets such as Turkey, India, Poland and Hungary, have helped it lift razor-blade sales by 2 billion a year since 1992.

To keep profits booming Zeien reckons Gillette has to pump out new products and persuade customers to switch to more expensive lines. Zeien runs his company more like a drug manufacturer than a maker of consumer products. He believes in short product cycles, and makes big investments in innovative products that he hopes will command premium prices.

Paine Webber's Andrew Shore, who earlier this year moved from a buy to a neutral recommendation on Gillette – because he could not see how it could maintain its profit momentum or justify a price of 26 times 1996 earnings – says: 'There are not too many acquisitions that could be better for Gillette. This one was so obvious that we all missed it'. Duracell, which last year had sales of $2.3 billion (up 11% from 1994) and net income of $254.6m (up 9%), will make batteries Gillette's top product after razors and blades, and reduce the revenue from blades from 39% to less than 30% of the total.

> The battery company has been another amazing success story. Henry Kravis, the head of KKR, bought Duracell in 1988 from Kraft after a fight with Teddy Forstmann, a rival financier, and two other bidders.
>
> Kravis persuaded 35 of Duracell's managers to buy, or take options over, 9.85% of the stock. With this strong incentive, they boosted cash flow by more than 50% in the first year after the buyout, and by nearly 20% per year thereafter. Their shares, worth $5 in 1988, have risen more than 11 times.
>
> Duracell is now America's top battery and globally ranks just behind Ever Ready (made by Ralston Purina, the cat and dog food maker). But heavy investments in new overseas plants and poor market conditions in Europe recently depressed the company's performance and share price, so KKR, which took it public in 1991 and retained 34%, decided to sell. [...]
>
> But Kravis does not intend to cash in his new Gillette shares. Like Buffett, he knows a winner when he sees one.
>
> Source: The Sunday Times, 15 September 1996. Copyright © 1996 The Times Newspaper Ltd. All Rights Reserved

Henry Kravis, head of KKR, who bought Duracell

The logic of this acquisition may not appear immediately obvious. However, the logic sits in the top-right box in Table 3.1 – 'Achieving efficiency in current operations' from scope economies. Gillette will sell Duracell's batteries through its existing global distribution network; batteries and razors are similar types of purchases and the definition of an economy of scope is:

'using a resource [a global distribution network for razors] acquired for one purpose for additional purposes [selling batteries] at little or no extra cost.'

3.5 SUMMARY

In this section we have covered some of the most relevant conceptual tools for the analysis of international strategy. You will be familiar with some of these, such as the value chain, scale and scope economies, and competitive advantage, from earlier in the course. However, we have been extending their application to the formulation and implementation of international strategy – our first objective for this book. We have also added some new concepts: comparative advantage within the 'diamond', 'configuration' and 'co-ordination' of geographically dispersed international value chains and sources of advantage from global, local or 'glocal' strategies. We will now consider these different types of international strategies and structures in more detail.

4 INTERNATIONAL INDUSTRIES AND INTERNATIONAL FIRMS

You should now read the remainder of the Set Book Chapter 14, pp. 350–61.

We have already discussed the objectives of international and global strategies in Sections 2.4 and 3.4. In this section we will first expand upon some of the driving forces underpinning the tensions between globalisation and national differentiation discussed by Grant and then provide a further commentary on the rise of the transnational as part of the continuing search for international organisation structures to match the complexity of evolving international strategies. Finally, this section will consider any special factors which may affect the international strategies of MNCs in the service sector.

4.1 TYPES OF INTERNATIONAL INDUSTRY

Since Levitt's seminal article (1983), globalisation has become a dominant theme in management literature. Indeed, the popularity of the concept has led to overuse and misuse, so that companies may speak of 'global' strategy when they actually mean 'international' and are speaking in a general sense of anything connected with doing business outside the domestic market. Indeed, Yip (1992) argued that most multinational companies lack an adequate global strategy, since they do not manage their worldwide businesses in a sufficiently integrated way. As we argued in Section 2.3, MNCs may also need to utilise different types of international strategies for different industries or sectors in which they do business, depending on the nature of the industry.

Bear in mind the key difference between international strategies:
- 'Multidomestic' (Porter, 1990, pp. 53–5) or 'multilocal' (Yip, 1992, p. 10) strategies treat competition in each country or region on a stand-alone basis, as Philips did.
- 'Global' strategies take an integrated approach across countries and regions, as Matsushita did.

For example, the US MNC Procter & Gamble may pursue a global strategy worldwide for disposable diapers, but a regional strategy in North America and Europe, and a multidomestic one in Asia-Pacific, for detergents. The reason for this is that diapers are used in a homogeneous way in all world markets (to protect babies' bottoms); it is therefore a genuine global product. Detergents are different in different parts of the world, since they have to cope with different fabrics, water, etc. (as discussed in the Electrolux case study).

4.1.1 Cultural homogenisation and the emergence of global markets

There has been a lengthy debate surrounding the argument that an increasing similarity (homogeneity) exists between groups of consumers within global markets. Much discussion has taken place over the opportunities for, and barriers to, standardisation of goods and services (Quelch and Hoff, 1986; Douglas and Wind, 1987). Markets are converging, and social, economic and cultural differences, including old-established differences in national tastes and preferences, diminishing.

Influences on cultural convergence include art, films, television, clothing, the Internet, ethnic foods, travel and popular music. Such developments are not confined to OECD (Organisation for Economic Co-operation and Development) countries. In India, for example, the market for consumer durables, once confined to a very small number of wealthy families, has grown at an unprecedented rate, reflecting the rise of a substantial middle class, now estimated to stand at approximately 20 per cent of a total population of over 900 million. Demand for international brands in India now makes it an attractive market for companies which already trade on a global basis. The relaxation of many of India's barriers to foreign trade and investment since 1992 has created a rapid expansion of multinational activity in the subcontinent.

Global market segments can provide the basis for a global strategy. The Italian retail chain Benetton has built its international strategy on the identification of a specific target market segment (leisurewear for 14–25 year olds) as a platform for global marketing. Certainly Benetton adapts such things as colour choice for different domestic markets, but such adaptation occurs around the standardised core of Benetton's 'one united product' for its target market segment worldwide, thus achieving significant economies of scale.

Standardisation does not therefore mean providing the same product in all countries, but offering local adaptations around a standardised core. Just as Benetton balances standardisation with some local adaptation of colours and store size, so Pizza Hut ensures standardisation across markets by operating a strict specification of product ingredients. However, the Pizza Hut concept is adapted to suit local needs in differing ways. Some elements of the menu (such as desserts) will vary, as will the way in which products are served to the customer. As Quelch and Hoff (1986) remarked, the relevant issue 'is not whether to go global but how to tailor the global marketing concept to fit each business'.

4.1.2 The global standardisation/adaptation debate

The standardisation/adaptation debate in international strategy questions how far it is appropriate to design, market and deliver standard products and services across national market boundaries, and how far adaptation to local market requirements (as in Pizza Hut) is mandatory. Douglas and Wind (1987) were early critics of the argument for global standardisation, calling it 'naive and oversimplistic'. Since then there have been waves of research and practice supporting globalisation, 'glocalisation' ('think global, act local') and transnational management (Bartlett and Ghoshal, 1989, 1993).

There is a lack of evidence of homogenisation. It has been argued by managers and academics alike that the differences both within and across countries are far greater than any similarities. There has also been a growth of intra-country fragmentation, leading to increased segmentation of domestic markets. Finally, developments in factory automation allowing flexible, lower cost, lower volume, high variety operations ('mass customisation') are challenging the economies of scale of standardisation by providing variety at low cost. The argument put forward here is that global strategies have become too focused on the benefits of standardisation, when the emphasis internationally is shifting from the global to the regional.

4.1.3 The advantages of global operations

Spreading operations across a number of different national markets can provide the opportunity to standardise the way in which the product or service is marketed to the consumer. Companies as diverse as Sony and Matsushita (both Japanese) in consumer electronics, Burger King (UK) and Kentucky Fried Chicken (US) in fast food, or Benetton (Italian) and IKEA (Swedish) in retailing, have developed their products and services to have universal appeal across global markets, allowing for more standardised marketing and distribution strategies for their products and services.

Substantial cost savings may be available. In advertising costs, for example, PepsiCo's savings from not producing a separate film for individual national markets has been estimated at $10 million per year. This figure is increased when indirect costs are added, for instance the speed of implementing a campaign, fewer overseas marketing staff, and management time which can be utilised elsewhere.

The restructuring of international supply chains for transportation and distribution has created opportunities for rethinking international logistics operations. Cost reductions, shorter journey times and dramatic technological developments in transportation have together created new international markets for products which previously had no shelf-life beyond local consumption. Container systems which use computer-controlled temperature, humidity and atmosphere levels have extended the geographic scope for such products as fresh fruit or flowers, just as surely as international information systems have created transparent 24-hour trading in financial products.

The possible benefits available from globalisation of operations may include any or all of the following: design, purchasing, manufacturing operations, packaging, distribution, marketing, advertising, customer service or software development – making possible standardised facilities, methodologies and procedures across locations. Companies may be able to benefit even if they are able to reconfigure in only one or two of these areas (as described in Section 3.3). Such a contingent approach allows flexibility between the two extremes of full global standardisation and complete local market responsiveness. Indeed both approaches may be used simultaneously to achieve the advantages to be had from global structuring of part of the product/service offering, while adapting or fine-tuning other parts of the same offering to closely match the needs of a particular local market.

This process of combining the advantages of both global and local operations has become known as 'glocalisation'. The experience of Kentucky Fried Chicken (KFC), an American international fast food chain, may illustrate the point. After its initial entry into the Japanese market KFC rapidly realised that it was necessary to make three specific changes to its international strategy. First, the product was of the wrong shape and size, since the Japanese prefer morsel-sized food. Second, the locations of the outlets had to be moved into crowded city eating areas and away from independent sites. Third, contracts for supply of appropriate quality chickens had to be negotiated locally, although KFC provided all technical advice and standards. After these adaptations, KFC have been successful in Japan. Similarly, Pampers disposable diapers (made by Procter & Gamble) were only successful in Japan after sizing downwards to accommodate smaller Japanese baby bottoms. Each of these adaptations was critical, yet the global strategy was unchanged in its essentials.

Global markets for culturally specific products. The hamburger (left) was once as culturally specific to the USA as sushi (right) is to Japan. The hamburger is now available almost everywhere with only the smallest concessions to local cultures. Similarly, the healthy image of Oriental food is helping it to make inroads into the fast food market in the West. (Source: *The Observer*, 2 March 1997)

Significant advantages of global trading should be associated with size (Chandler, 1990). Economies of scale provide not just lower unit costs, but also potentially greater bargaining power over all elements in the company's value chain. Economies of scope can allow for the sharing of resources across products, markets and businesses. Such resources may be both tangible, such as buildings, technology or sales forces, or intangible, such as expert knowledge or teamworking skills (refer back to Table 3.1).

4.1.4   The globalisation of brands

Branding is a useful illustration of economies of scope available from global strategies.

Philips, the European consumer electronics and white goods manufacturer, merged its white goods business with US domestic appliance manufacturer Whirlpool in 1989. Whirlpool dual-branded its products 'Philips Whirlpool' until 1992, when the Philips name was dropped. This approach was adopted in order to give European consumers enough time to become aware of the Whirlpool brand in association with Philips's strong brand reputation. By 1992, Whirlpool's internal figures showed that awareness of its brand across Europe had reached 97 per cent of the Philips level. This was deemed sufficient to move on to the next phase of the strategy to benefit from rationalisation of the global brand. Another well-known example in the UK in the early 1990s was the rebranding of the chocolate bar Marathon, which was renamed Snickers in line with its worldwide brand, thus allowing economies of scale in packaging and marketing.

An increasing number of MNCs are standardising their brands to send a consistent worldwide message and to take greater advantage of media opportunities by promoting one brand, one packaging and uniform positioning across markets. Rather than a patchwork quilt of local brands in local markets, the owners of international brands increasingly want simplified international brand portfolios to realise potential scale and scope economies. Many of these local brands have been nurtured lovingly over the long-term by high advertising spend and careful handling and are often held in great affection by their local population. Despite this, they are likely to be swept away. In the UK, Access was the local brand for Mastercard, but was virtually unknown in the rest of the world. In 1996 Mastercard negotiated with the four UK clearing banks which owned a stake in it to regain control and rebrand the card as Mastercard. While Access was a strong brand in a national market, Mastercard is the global brand for a global company; the pressure for replacing Access became overwhelming.

Companies increasingly feel that they have to unite behind key brands, and rationalise products, brands and the advertising agencies handling their accounts. Focusing on fewer, stronger brands is seen as the best way of coping with fierce competition, from other brands and private-label products, as well as getting the best value from expensive investments in advertising (as in the PepsiCo example in Section 4.1.3).

4.1.5 The impact of regional trading blocs

Overall growth in international trade is policed by the World Trade Organisation, the successor to the General Agreement on Tariffs and Trade (GATT). Moves towards the liberalisation of international trade go hand-in-hand with its restructuring into larger and larger regional trading blocs. This means that regional strategies are of increasing significance for MNCs.

Recently, much international strategy has been aimed at restructuring and rationalisation at a regional rather than a global level. This has reflected the build-up of regional trading blocs in the 'Triad' (three major trading regions) worldwide: NAFTA (USA, Canada and Mexico, plus an application from Chile) in North America; ASEAN and APEC in Asia-Pacific; and the European Union (EU), which having expanded from its original six members was up to fifteen by 1996 and had another fourteen applications for membership outstanding for consideration from the countries of Northern and Eastern Europe. An enlarged NAFTA may well gradually extend to include much of Central and South America. Already there are many agreements in place in South America, such as the Andean pact between Venezuela, Colombia and Bolivia, or the Mercosur Free Trade Association between Brazil, Argentina, Uruguay and Paraguay. Since 1987, the USA has signed sixteen 'framework' agreements with Latin American countries. The groundwork exists for a pan-American trading bloc embracing all the Americas. Intra-regional trade between Japan, Hong Kong, South Korea, the five ASEAN countries (Singapore, Malaysia, Indonesia, the Philippines and Thailand), Australia and New Zealand, has grown to 43 per cent of the region's total exports. International trade and international investment are both exhibiting faster intra-regional (within each region) than inter-regional (across regions) growth. These developments are captured in Figure 4.1.

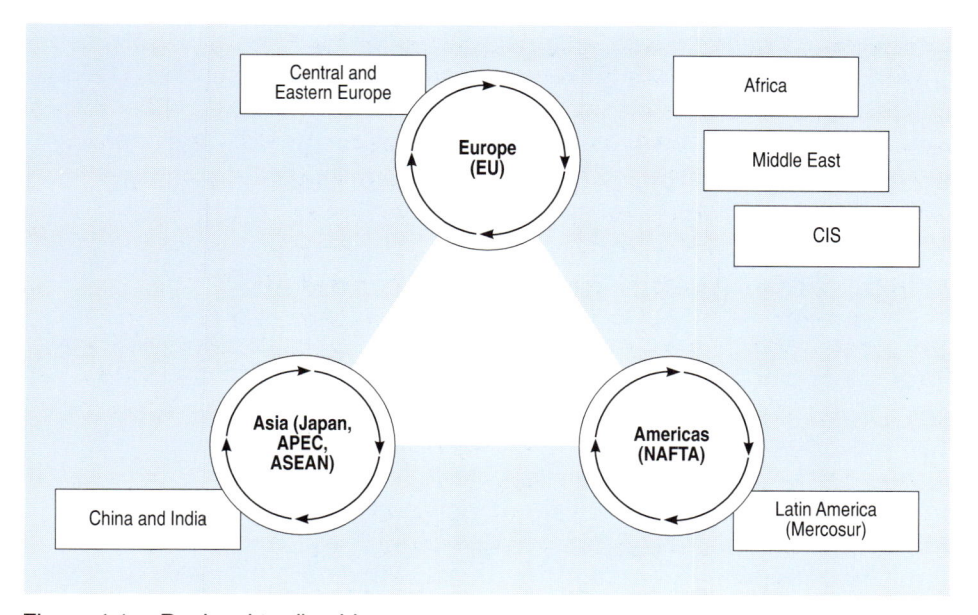

Figure 4.1   Regional trading blocs

Examples of developments in regional strategy include PepsiCo of the USA – a major operator of restaurants and provider of beverages and snacks internationally. It had given local divisional managers autonomy in managing their national businesses, to grow the local markets. In September 1994, the company announced that it was centralising purchasing across all its various European businesses. PepsiCo and its divisions Pizza Hut and KFC were identified as having many items in common, such as the large volumes of cardboard which Pizza Hut uses for its cartons and PepsiCo for its soft drinks trays. Volume savings are expected from sugar, cooking oil, flour, packaging materials and even advertising costs. By so doing, PepsiCo expected to save $100 million per annum, which represented 5 per cent of its annual European operating costs of $2 billion. If successful, these regional policies will be copied for North and South America and Asia-Pacific.

Nike is a US sports shoe and clothing manufacturing company which markets its products worldwide. In Europe it had traditionally utilised local national warehousing to supply retailers. Nike is replacing more than twenty national warehouses with a single European distribution centre located in Belgium. Developing a single European distribution hub follows the company's successful centralisation of its American operations to a single hub in Memphis. Such regional concentration of warehousing and distribution is intended to help Nike reduce inventory, avoid duplication, and stock a wider range of its products centrally, so reducing cost while improving availability.

The European insurance market has historically been highly fragmented. This has enabled large price differentials to flourish between national markets: for example, a similar policy could cost in Portugal three times what it cost in France. Since 1994, the European Union has developed a series of 'framework directives' which have gradually opened up the European markets to cross-border competition. These directives have brought about two basic changes: first, they allow companies to sell policies anywhere in Europe based on the regulations in their domestic market; second, they remove the need to submit cross-border policies to local offices for approval. The impact of these changes is expected to be increased industry-wide competition undermining the hitherto protected position and profitability of some national providers. Cross-border market penetration using lower-cost channels such as direct telephone sales had already begun in the 1990s. However, market differences such as local tax regimes, cultural preferences for different types of insurance products, legal factors and incidence of different types of claims will ensure that cross-border entrants will still have to meet country-specific requirements for the foreseeable future.

4.1.6 How global are 'global' markets?

Local Asian markets have caused difficulties for Rupert Murdoch's News Corporation empire which owns the STAR TV satellite network. STAR claims to broadcast to about 53.7 million households across Asia and to have a viewing audience estimated at about 220 million. News Corporation's strategy, after taking control of the network in 1993, was to aim at the top 5 per cent of television viewers by providing English-language programmes. This strategy was soon abandoned in favour of supplying programmes broadcast in the local language. Its original global segmentation strategy was based on the assumption that a homogeneous television product could be sold across Asia. However, it quickly became evident that advertising depends on ratings and ratings depend on providing programmes that people in Asia want to watch. This commercial logic has driven STAR to local programming and a regional management structure.

Although China is consuming more and more Western products, it is difficult to judge the positioning for each product. For example, chewing gum is so popular because it is one of the few Western pleasures within the financial reach of Chinese parents. Packaging and distribution channels also have local characteristics. For example, hair shampoos are sold predominantly in sachets rather than in bottles, because people are paid weekly and prefer to make smaller weekly expenditures. The most favoured distribution outlet for shampoo is barber shops rather than grocery stores, since going to the hairdresser in China is a social occasion.

Similarly, McDonald's took 14 years to extend its chain to Russia. Negotiations with the Soviet authorities were notoriously slow, and fundamentals, such as the legal ownership of outlets, difficult to establish. No supply chain existed for sourcing the raw materials for hamburgers and french fries. The company had to go to extraordinary lengths to create a reliable supply chain of appropriate quality ingredients for its product. These included agreements with farm co-operatives to grow the right strain of potato needed for McDonald's french fries, and importing American bull sperm to ensure that Russian beef herds yielded the correct beef quality expected in the hamburgers. Even on opening, aspects of the service were perplexing to local customers, including the menu itself, since the notions of choice and availability were not familiar to the Russian consumer.

4.1 7 Regional or global?

Many successful product or service innovations have been a result of ideas observed elsewhere. A presence in international markets creates antennae for gathering market intelligence, mentioned by many international companies as one of the most important benefits of a varied international presence and a factor which is leading to a rethinking of centralised global operations (as we discussed in relation to Matsushita).

4.2 TYPES OF INTERNATIONAL FIRM

In Chapter 14 of the Set Book, you will have read about different organisation structures for different types of international strategy, to match different sets of market and industry conditions. We will now elaborate further on one of these types: the transnational.

4.2.1 The transnational

Developed first in the work of Bartlett and Ghoshal (1989), the transnational is probably best understood as a state of mind rather than an organisation structure. It is a state of mind which is adaptable and which sees efficiency, across international boundaries, as something that companies achieve through the ability to learn. As an approach to meeting international objectives, it places great strains on international business managers.

Figure 4.2 illustrates the difference between the two dominant organisational structural types in international strategy: centralised hubs (top left) and decentralised federations (bottom right) and the transnational organisation – defined here as an *integrated network*. The diagrammatic representation highlights two particular differences in the new form compared with the old: multilateral communications between all levels and layers, replacing 'top-down' or 'bottom-up'; and the idea

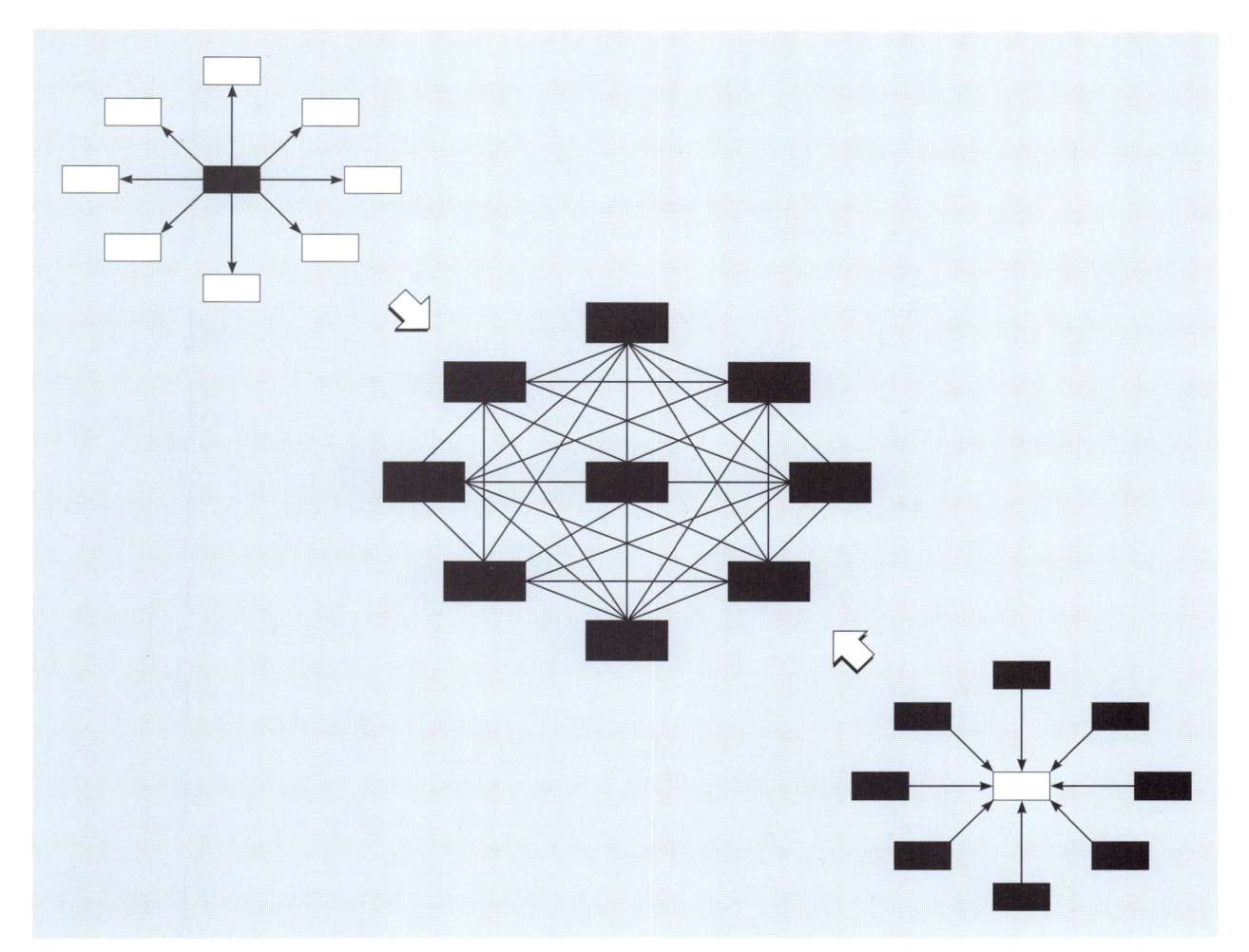

Figure 4.2 Emergence of the 'integrated network': distributed resources, differentiated roles and responsibilities, shared influence and decision-making

that resources, responsibilities and decision-making are dispersed across all types of units, not just concentrated either at the centre or at the periphery (refer back also to Table 2.1). This is what Bartlett and Ghoshal (1993) mean by 'beyond the M-form', where 'M' stands for 'multidivisional'. Instead, an 'N-form' organisation appears to be emerging, with 'N' standing for 'network'. They stress the importance of 'co-ordinating mechanisms', with the role of senior management being to provide shared corporate purpose, similar to the points made by Senge (1990) in the Reader article for Book 9. They use the company ABB, which you may remember from Book 8, as their illustrative case.

You should now read the article by Bartlett and Ghoshal in the Course Reader.

In this article, Bartlett and Ghoshal are attempting to develop a managerial theory of the firm, able to incorporate the management of high degrees of complexity and flexibility, with new ways of integrating activities and resources across borders. Their approach integrates structure, systems and processes for international organisations. Most importantly, they are able to explain clearly what such restructuring processes would mean in practice. A critical appraisal of the efforts of organisations and managers to achieve these complex organisational objectives in reality is contained in the article in Box 4.1.

BOX 4.1 'THE DISCREET CHARM OF THE MULTICULTURAL MULTINATIONAL'

[...] As a slogan, globalisation is the stalest of buns. [...] In the 1980s 'globalisation' was the buzzword that launched a thousand strategies. For years, management gurus have pontificated on 'the borderless corporation.' Yet today's globalising firms are much more significant than their predecessors, for two reasons.

One is that there are so many of them. [...] The world now boasts a total of 37,000 transnational companies, which control about a third of all private-sector assets, and enjoy worldwide sales of about $5.5 trillion – slightly less than America's GDP last year. [...]

The second thing that is different about the current round of globalisation could change this. Its aim is to pit all a firm's resources, wherever they are, against its competitors. That means not only moving production facilities around to benefit from the quickest brains or the cheapest hands, but also breaking down internal barriers to the free movement of people and, particularly, of ideas.

The 'multicultural multinational', as some are calling this new animal, is based on two ideas about modern business life. First, that innovation is the key to success. An organisation that relies on one culture for its ideas and treats foreign subsidiaries as dumb production-colonies might as well hire subcontractors. Second, that technology is slowly making the world seem smaller. It is now possible for software writers in Bangalore and Palo Alto to work together on programs, even if the programs then have to be specially tailored for local markets.

This has big implications for company management. AT & T admits the global reorganisation accounted for most of the colossal $347m it paid in fees to consultants last year. Gillette, an American consumer-goods firm, likens its new global management system to operating in 'over 500 states'. Ford has just embarked on a colossal plan to turn itself into a borderless firm.

Matsushita's president, Yoichi Morishita, recently warned the Japanese electronics giant's managers that in order 'to become a truly global company, we have to have diversity in top management'. Sony now aims to give the top job in each of its subsidiaries to a manager from the host country: since 1989 it has appointed three foreigners to its board of directors.

European firms have done better. But they are also more realistic about their progress. 'There are very few multicultural multinationals; the truly global multicultural company does not yet exist,' David de Pury, co-chairman of Asea Brown Boveri (ABB), a Swedish-Swiss electrical-engineering giant, flatly informed a recent international management symposium at St Gallen in Switzerland. He pointed out that few multinationals produce more than 20% of their goods and services outside their immediate or wider home market; that most boards come predominantly from one culture; and that few multinationals are ready to let their shareholder base become as global as their business.

This dismissal is the more striking in coming from ABB, a firm with a board of eight directors from four different nationalities; an executive committee of eight people from five countries; English as its corporate language; and financial results reported in dollars. Perhaps only Royal Dutch/Shell – another European giant of mixed parentage, which has some 38 nationalities in its London head office – can claim to have advanced so far down the multicultural route. What chance is there then for big American or Japanese firms that think globalisation simply means having occasional board meetings in London or Paris?

That illusory goal

Would-be multicultural multinationals are struggling to solve a dilemma that has bedevilled their predecessors: the clash between global standardisation and local roots. The first offers huge advantages of both scale and speed. ABB reckons that makers of standardised products can cut unit costs by 20–30% by running fewer plants, buying from fewer suppliers and reducing duplication. Global firms can also shift huge volumes of goods at high speed – an invaluable trick in a world in which the life-cycle of goods is shortening by the day.

But local knowledge can help Davids slay Goliaths; and ignorance can fell Goliaths even if there are no Davids around. Procter & Gamble endured a series of painful product failures because of its (now abandoned) policy of imposing managers from headquarters on overseas subsidiaries. Nowadays big firms seek local help not only to tailor ideas to local markets (McDonald's restaurants now serve Teriyaki burgers in Tokyo and wine in Lyons) but also to get access to local expertise.

A soon-to-be-published study of patents granted to multinationals between 1920 and 1990 by John Cantwell, an economist at Reading University, shows just how far big firms have to go in terms of persuading foreign subsidiaries to think as well as they distribute. By his reckoning, only 9% of the patents granted to American multinationals in the 1980's were for work done by overseas operations; for European firms, the ratio was 30%. [...]

Organising workers is difficult ...

The need to combine global clout with local savvy leaves would-be multicultural multinationals with two tricky challenges: one organisational, the other motivational. On the organisational side, a few brave firms, notably Ford, have pushed ahead with restructuring themselves along product lines.

Caterpillar's 'plant with a future' is also built around an integrated global-production process. A new survey of foreign-subsidiary managers around the world by America's Conference Board concludes that many of them 'are losing authority over production decisions.'

Most multinationals, however, have adopted matrix structures, with each unit reporting simultaneously to a product-group headquarters and a country headquarters. In theory, this means that managers can make decisions without regard for national borders – but only if they want to. Thus ABB, which uses a matrix system (and usually makes much of its global spread), presented itself as a Swiss company, uniquely familiar with Alpine terrain and temperament, when it came to tendering for a contract with the Swiss federal railway.

Others have had less-happy experiences. Digital Equipment recently announced that it was dumping its matrix system in a global restructuring which will cost $1 billion and 20,000 jobs. [...] So has Citibank, which also discarded its highly publicised experiments with dual reporting. [...]

The organisations that have so far been best at exploiting local variations are not in fact the big multinationals but smaller network-weaving companies, which exploit different clusters of specialist firms. One example is Nike, an American shoe maker, which subcontracts the manufacture of its athletic shoes and clothing to 40 separate locations, mostly in Asia. Designs are sent to a plant in Taiwan; a prototype is then built; and the final plans are faxed to subcontractors throughout Asia.

Older, larger multinationals have tried to perform the same trick through alliances – but, like networks, they are extremely difficult to manage on a global scale. AT&T's alliance with Philips in Europe was touted as a good example of two rivals joining forces to swap technology for access to a local market. But the alliance never lived up to expectations – mainly because the firms failed to understand each other's strategic objectives. Managing such vaguely defined relationships is difficult enough at the best of times, distance, language and culture bring added complications. [...]

... inspiring them is even harder

Motivating diversified workforces is in some ways even harder. On the one hand many companies are trying to become less ethnocentric. Philips, for instance, has begun to open its top ranks in Holland to non-Dutchmen. Many big firms, such as Citibank and Royal Dutch/Shell, rotate managers. They are also redesigning incentive systems to reward employees who help sister companies. Similarly, IBM is introducing performance measures to reward managers for co-operating with colleagues around the world.

However, diverse companies also need to have a common sense of purpose. McDonald's issues its employees worldwide with an operating manual as thick as a phone-book, which lays down the law on everything from how to greet customers to how to clean the lavatories, and also sends its more promising managers to one of four hamburger universities. Unilever brings hundreds of managers from around the world to its training centres in Britain. Apple Computer has a tradition of holding annual jamborees in places such as Hawaii. Smaller multinationals may be cosier: Richard Branson invites employees of his Virgin empire to parties at his house.

In the end, running a company in a borderless world is about trying to resolve a number of apparent contradictions. Firms have to be responsive to national needs, yet seek to exploit know-how on a worldwide basis, while, all the time,

> striving to produce and distribute goods globally as efficiently as possible. Many companies manage to achieve one, maybe even two, of these objectives. It is hard to think of any company that has yet managed to balance all three simultaneously.
>
> Source: The Economist, *30 July 1994*

We shall now look at how these issues are affecting service industries.

4.3 INTERNATIONAL COMPETITION IN SERVICES

Service industries are those whose output is not a physical good or product but an intangible 'experience'. This underpins an essential difference in the significance of globalisation in services as opposed to manufacturing. Manufacturing is concerned with the most effective ways of moving the product to the market. In service industries, globalisation means that a mobile customer base (often literally mobile – the tourist, the shopper, the business traveller) experiences a similar service wherever they go.

Service delivery is about controlling the quality of the offering at the point of sale to the customer. In service industries the customer can move to the product. American Express labels its core charge card (and travellers cheque and travel shop) business: 'travel related services' (TRS). The TRS market is the international (mainly business/corporate) traveller. The aim is to provide a standard quality service to the targeted customer, wherever that service is taken up. Similarly, the international hotel chains (Hilton, Sheraton, Inter-continental) undertake to make the traveller's experience of Tokyo, Cape Town, Manila or Sydney, as similar as possible. The expectation of the customer is for consistency of service levels in any location worldwide.

The debate on global competition has given relatively little attention to service industries. The literature on global strategy (Yip, 1989, 1992) has taken its evidence overwhelmingly from manufacturing industry. In the last completed Uruguay Round of GATT, no international agreement was reached to reduce service trade barriers. Such an agreement is being addressed by its successor, the World Trade Organisation, and will lead to further internationalisation of services. In services it is often the customer who internationalises first, with the service company following to keep important clients. This was the main trigger factor for much of the concentration in the advertising industry worldwide. Firms such as Omnicom, WPP or Interpublic needed to build international networks to serve international clients requiring the delivery of global campaigns. Large service firms are developing the ability to standardise and replicate facilities, methodologies and procedures across locations.

Service growth has partly come as a consequence of organisational trends towards delayering, outsourcing and downsizing. Specialist service suppliers are replacing service provision previously carried out in-house. Firms such as EDS, the US technology and facilities management company, have grown rapidly, nationally and internationally, as external suppliers of information technology (IT) design and management for client organisations. Specialisation and standardisation are leading to high-quality provision at lower cost to the client company or customer, while the branding of services has become an important guarantee of quality and consistency around the world.

4.3.1 Managing 'intangibles' across borders

Service industries have some important characteristics which distinguish them from manufacturing industries. Among the most widely recognised are those of 'intangibility' of the service offering and the simultaneous production and consumption of the service (Sasser *et al.*, 1978). The nature of a service offering may be best understood as an 'experience' or 'outcome'. The successful management of a service business thus becomes the management of the quality of the experience for the customer or client. It is this quality of customer experience, often known as 'the moment of truth', by which service quality is measured (Normann, 1984; Carlzon, 1987). This would be equally true of a firm of accountants as for a restaurant. Thus for service industries, control of the offering at the transaction point with the customer or client is critical. When the service network is extended globally, the management of outcomes for the customer faces obvious quality control problems in accurately reproducing the service concept in different cultural, political and economic environments and ensuring consistency in the quality of the offering at all transaction points. Most large service firms have met these requirements for international consistency through standardisation. However, issues such as staff training are critical in international service firms since it is these front-line staff who are responsible for the quality of the customer's experience.

4.3.2 Scale and scope in services

You should now read the article by Segal-Horn in the Course Reader.

Activity 4.1

Having read the article, explain the difference between 'back-office' and 'front-office' activities in services.

Why is this distinction so significant for international services?

Discussion

'Front-office' describes those activities which come into contact with the customer; 'back-office' are the operational activities which can be decoupled from the customer. The significance of this distinction in international strategy terms for service MNCs is that the larger the proportion of 'back-office' value chain activities in the service that can be decoupled from the location of the customer, the greater the potential for reconfiguring the organisation's value chain and securing scale and scope advantages in the same way as manufacturing MNCs. If most activities of a service organisation cannot be decoupled from the customer in this way, then strategic flexibility remains low and the costs, risks and service delivery problems for an international strategy remain high.

The separation of back-office and front-office activities (see Figure 19.4 in the Course Reader article), combined with the standardisation of many back-office processing functions, has created the opportunity for breaking out of the requirement for simultaneous consumption and production of a service. This allows for the reconfiguration of service value chains which can be disaggregated (just as for manufacturers). Parts of the activity may be located geographically for optimum scale, scope or cost advantage. For example a company like VISA International has a geographically dispersed value chain whereby all its worldwide back-office data transactions (e.g. card clearances) are handled by just two global transaction centres in Japan and the USA. These types of international configuration for services are technology-dependent.

Economies of scale and economies of scope were concepts developed largely on the basis of evidence gathered from manufacturing industries. Potential sources of economies of scale and scope in services are helpful in providing guidelines for the likely patterns of future development and investment in international service firms.

In the next section we shall look at some of the corporate strategy issues affecting international strategy.

5 INTERNATIONAL STRATEGY DEVELOPMENT

In Section 2, Figure 2.2 provided a decision-tree for deciding upon a preferred route for international growth. The path through the decision tree tells you that if there are no barriers to free trade, you should simply export. If there are barriers to trade and there is also a risk of dissipation of proprietary knowledge, then FDI is called for. If there are barriers to trade but no risk to proprietary knowledge, then license. Where resources are limited and risk of dissipation of proprietary knowledge is containable, then strategic alliances are appropriate. Strategic alliances are a point midway between markets and hierarchies. Many international strategies are now realised through strategic alliances.

5.1 STRATEGIC ALLIANCES AND JOINT VENTURES

From time to time in earlier Books (6, 8 and 10) mention has been made of network organisations, virtual organisations, quasi-integration, co-operative strategies and alliances. In this section on strategic alliances the level of analysis will change. We will focus not on theory but on understanding the management and operational issues to which these types of network structures give rise. The what, why and how of alliances will be addressed:

What are they?

What are they for?

Why are they so popular?

How should they be managed?

A strategic alliance exists whenever two or more independent organisations co-operate in the development, manufacture or sale of products or services (Hennart, 1988). A dramatic growth of such cross-border co-operation between organisations has occurred since the mid-1980s. Alliances will inevitably involve additional costs and have inherent disadvantages. The frustrations of working in partnership may be considerable. They may include the need for trade-offs and compromise; the need to take account of partners' cultures, attitudes and expectations; loss of direct control over invested capital; restrictions on freedom to act in one's sole interest, as opposed to the interest of the alliance; such commitments may limit opportunities elsewhere; the possible need to disclose proprietary knowledge. Given all these problems, why are alliances so popular?

Stimuli for creating partnerships may be both external and internal. The increasing globalisation of international business in many sectors, coupled with competitive pressures, creates a need for partners to ameliorate resource shortfalls, to gain time, to improve competitive position, or to bring together distinctive competencies from several partners.

These reasons may be summarised as:

- faster penetration and exploitation of key markets and other opportunities in which there is a substantial probability that organic (internal) growth will be too slow
- where alliances are broadly structured, such partnerships create options to develop in major new strategic directions which otherwise might not be possible for one partner alone
- the potential payoffs to collaboration are felt to offset the costs and risks of collaboration
- immediate access to markets, to resources, to funds, to skills and technologies, to rights
- cost-reduction through increased economies of scale
- synergies through blending complementary strengths or assets
- a need for complex resource bundles
- safety by spreading financial risk, sharing novelty risks, reducing political risk, reducing market volatility, rationalising standards, influencing new industry developments
- a way of building defences.

5.1.1 Management issues affecting strategic alliances

Despite the popularity of international co-operative enterprises, or strategic alliances as they are usually called, the record of running successful alliances is somewhat mixed. The success of an alliance may lie more in its management than in the circumstances of its initial creation. According to Harrigan (1984):

> Alliances fail because operating managers do not make them work, not because contracts are poorly written.

Managers from partner companies often come from different national and corporate cultures, and have difficulty in understanding or approving of their new allies' ways of operating. In addition, they may have been trained to operate in hierarchically organised firms and are somewhat disadvantaged when faced with the need to act through consensus. The following section will focus on such operational rather than strategic issues.

You should now listen to the Audio tape 'Strategic alliances', an interview with David Faulkner.

Faulkner's research (1994) suggested that the successful long-term management of international strategic alliances was less reliant upon the economic benefits the partners receive from the alliance, than upon the attitudes of the partners towards each other and the degree to which they adopt a positive learning philosophy, thus enabling the alliance to evolve. Faulkner's results accord closely with those of Mohr and Spekman (1994).

Faulkner found that four factors played a key role in the successful management of alliances: positive attitudes between the partners, clear organisational arrangements for the alliance, a philosophy of organisational learning and congruent long-term goals.

Positive partner attitudes towards the alliance included:

(a) a sensitive attitude to national and corporate cultural differences

(b) strong commitment by top and lower-level management in the partner companies

(c) mutual trust.

Alliance management is therefore not just about systems and goals, but also about attitudes and interpersonal relationships.

Clear organisational arrangements need to be set up in an alliance if it is to be managed effectively including:

(a) the establishment of clear dispute resolution mechanisms

(b) in a joint-venture alliance, clear authority vested in the chief executive of the joint venture

(c) an appropriate legal form

(d) a 'divorce mechanism' agreed at the outset, and

(e) processes for wide dissemination of information within the alliance.

A learning philosophy. Alliances set up with the prime purpose of substituting for skills or products in which a partner is deficient tend to have limited scope for development. For an alliance to succeed in the long term it needs to evolve through the partners constantly seeking new things to do together. In essence it is a learning arrangement between companies with different things to teach and learn (Hamel, 1991). Faulkner uses the alliance between the two automobile companies Rover (UK) and Honda (Japan) to illustrate the importance of organisational learning from cross-border alliances. His research has shown that the most successful long-term alliances are those in which the partners learn to learn from each other, so that their mutual agenda shifts and develops as the alliance matures. In the early days of the alliance, Rover wanted only rapid development of a mid-range saloon model. It was not until much later, when learning became Rover's primary objective, that the company experienced dramatic broader benefit from the alliance in terms of improved production methods, design, training and so on.

Congruent long-term goals. Long-term goals and objectives of the partners need not necessarily dovetail. Clearly those of Rover and Honda did not. However, the objectives must not actually conflict, otherwise the alliance partners may have difficulty in developing consensus for a particular course of action.

5.1.2 Types of alliance

There are many different forms of alliance; Faulkner gives some definitions and examples:

- *Joint ventures* – defined as Company A and Company B setting up Company C to achieve a commonly agreed purpose, e.g.:
    - ICI Pharma was set up in 1972 by ICI Pharmaceuticals (UK) (60 per cent) and Sumitomo Chemicals (Japan) (40 per cent) to produce and market certain ICI pharmaceutical products in Japan. ICI provided the product specification, Sumitomo manufactured the products and achieved Japanese registration for them. The joint venture company ICI Pharma sold and distributed them.
- *Collaborations* – defined as flexible alliances between companies in which a new corporate form is not necessarily created (e.g. Rover/Honda). Joint ventures involve the creation of separate companies; collaborations do not. Barney (1996) also distinguishes between

equity and non-equity alliances, where partners do or do not have equity (or cross-equity) investments in each other.
- Courtaulds/Nippon Paint was set up in 1976 because Courtaulds (UK) needed a reliable Japanese company to service it and its customers' needs in Japan. Nippon wished to rise in the league table of Japanese marine paint companies, and regarded an alliance with Courtaulds, the acknowledged world leader in the area, as a significant step in helping it achieve this aim.
- Royal Bank of Scotland/Banco Santander (Spain), set up in 1988, was a partial union of two medium-sized national banks in the face of the expected Europeanisation of the banking industry. The partners own a small minority of each other's shares. The alliance operates on many fronts, including joint ventures in Germany and Gibraltar, and a consortium for money transfer covering a number of European countries.

- *Consortia* – alliances between more than two partners:
  - International Digital Corporation is a joint venture consortium as it operates through a separate company. It was formed in pursuit of Cable & Wireless's (UK) strategy of building a global presence in the telecoms market. Given their limited size in global terms, development through strategic alliances has been an obvious route. Since the Japanese market is important for this strategy, C&W determined in 1986 to obtain a licence to become the second Japanese international carrier. In order to do this, they set up a consortium company (International Digital Corporation) which included some major Japanese corporations in order to achieve credibility with the Japanese government. Toyota and C Itoh each hold 17 per cent of the equity; about 20 Japanese shareholders share the remainder. After lengthy negotiations with the Japanese government, the consortium was successful in obtaining its international carrier licence.

5.1.3 Making alliances work

There are difficulties involved not just in setting up international strategic alliances, but also in maintaining positive co-operative attitudes as the alliance progresses.

'Boundary-spanning' is a critical aspect of alliances, and the skill with which it is carried out seems to have considerable impact on the success of the alliance. A 'gateway' system is one in which all communications, at least in the early months of an alliance, pass through the office of only one 'gatekeeper' in each partner company, in order to avoid the risk of misunderstandings, through the proliferation of contacts. Courtaulds/Nippon Paint have adopted a form of 'gateway' system which gives a degree of focus to the contacts between the companies. The mission of the 'gateway' executives is boundary-spanning (Killing, 1992). The 'gatekeeper' is normally a senior executive in each company who directly manages the interfaces between the companies, and is kept informed of all contacts and hence, by implication, any areas of (potential) dispute. By a careful selection of appropriate boundary-spanners, and by gradually increasing areas of involvement as the partners get to know each other, the effects of organisational incompatibilities may be reduced.

The most successful alliances have usually agreed at formation upon a formula for their dissolution: a 'divorce' procedure. This can help reduce anxiety about the cost of potential failure. The ill-fated joint venture in the 1980s between Pirelli (Italy) and Dunlop (UK) almost destroyed the partners in its wake.

The diffusion of knowledge gained from exposure to another company takes us back to the concept of the learning organisation (see the article by Senge in the Course Reader) discussed in Books 6, 8 and 9. A common alliance objective is to encourage the absorption of know-how, embedded knowledge and tacit routines from the partner. The limited objective of the early days of the Rover/Honda relationship (filling a gap in the Rover product line) developed into Rover's adoption of the Honda philosophy of 'continuous learning', as their agenda of joint activities grew. It set up a company (The Rover Learning Business Limited) to reinforce this approach. Rover claimed that much of the benefit they received from their alliance with Honda was through information dissemination within Rover, and the consequent organisational learning that has taken place, for example in team-working. Obviously all of these partnership benefits were threatened with destruction by the decision of Rover's parent company (British Aerospace) to sell Rover to BMW of Germany (a direct competitor in some sectors of the world car market) in 1994, as part of its review of its corporate portfolio.

Another issue of knowledge management is that relating to unintended transfers of knowledge. Hamel *et al.* (1989) make the point that Westerners are far less discreet than many of their Japanese alliance partners, who are far less likely to share proprietary information in a fit of openness, enthusiasm or pride of achievement. Westerners are more used to an open research culture; their Japanese partners receive more of their training from their employers and consider themselves corporate team members first. They quote one Japanese manager as saying: 'We don't feel any need to reveal what we know. It is not an issue of pride for us. If we're patient we usually learn what we want to know.'

Many alliances are set up for short-term gains in order to deal with temporary situations such as resource deficiencies or lack of market knowledge. Specific short-term objectives may be perfectly satisfactory. For example, Cable & Wireless admit that their Japanese partners all have differing agendas and that the consortium cannot be expected to remain stable over time. They are not unhappy with this since their basic objective was the new opportunities arising from developing a reputation in Japan as a good corporate citizen. Goals, which may have been congruent at the outset, may subsequently conflict, often as a result of the success of the alliance. Although Courtaulds wants Nippon Paint to continue to represent it in Japan, Nippon has been so successful that it is now in a position to pursue longer-term objectives to develop an independent global competitive position.

If nothing else, this demonstrates the degree to which the management of an alliance involves constant negotiation to find overlaps between goals, rather than to clarify totally congruent goals. As Kanter (1988) says, in alliances consensus-building replaces decision-taking. The potential problem of conflicting objectives is ever present in alliances, since perhaps their key characteristic is the wish of the partners to obtain the advantages of joint activity, while retaining their individual autonomy. A substantial contribution to success must therefore depend upon this quality of 'mutual forbearance' (Powell, 1990).

Activity 5.1

Having read this section on strategic alliances, to what extent would you view such co-operative strategies as confined to the private sector? Can you think of examples of similar arrangements between not-for-profit organisations? What might have caused any such developments?

Discussion

Examples of cross-border alliances or joint ventures between public sector organisations or not-for-profit organisations are numerous. We need only think of such organisations as Interpol – an international policing joint venture; the co-operative alliances practised by such charities as the Red Cross and Médecins du Monde for particular crises around the world; joint rescue operations mounted by governments in disaster situations such as earthquake, flood, famine or displacement of refugees. The reasons for such alliances are the same as in commercial situations: resource gaps or complementarities; speed of response; local market knowledge, and so on.

5.2 MERGERS AND ACQUISITIONS

Alongside the popularity of alliances, mergers and acquisitions remain another traditional route for entering new markets, acquiring instant market share, adding new (or exploiting more fully existing) capabilities, or sharing resources. In fact, any of the range of causes and objectives for alliances that were listed in Section 5.1 may equally well be applied to reasons for seeking mergers or acquisitions. They are different means to the same ends. One difference between the alliance route and the merger or acquisition route is cost. Unlike alliances, mergers and acquisitions have prior transaction and purchasing costs. In fact, alliances are a way of rapidly acquiring additional assets and resources without having to pay for them, or paying indirectly rather than directly. It must be emphasised that these indirect costs may be very heavy.

5.2.1 Divestment, demerger and withdrawal

It would be inappropriate to conclude this section without reference to the frequent need to divest, as well as acquire, in order to prune the corporate portfolio of the MNC (as British Aerospace did with Rover). A recent further development is that of the demerger: a voluntary splitting up of businesses within a corporate portfolio deemed to be worth more separated than together, as ICI did with ICI (agrichemicals) and Zeneca (pharmaceuticals), usually because the businesses are deemed to require different types of management and resource, a perceived lack of which may be holding down the share price. A different example is that of the tobacco corporations, whose unpopularity with some investors and consumers is affecting the value of other businesses within their portfolios. Philip Morris (US-based owner of the Marlborough brand of cigarettes) suffers this effect on its food business. British American Tobacco (BAT) suffers this effect on its financial businesses (Eagle Star).

5.2.2 International strategy development: the Electrolux/Zanussi acquisition revisited

In order to explore the corporate strategy implications of mergers and acquisitions within the context of international strategy, we will return to the Electrolux/Zanussi acquisition encountered in Book 3 as a worked case. This time, however, instead of using the case to explore the Electrolux experience of, and skills at, the acquisition management process, we will be looking at the Zanussi acquisition as part of the development of an international strategy for Electrolux in the context of the change and development in the white goods (domestic appliances) industry worldwide. This acquisition is what will enable Electrolux as a company to implement its global competitive strategy for sustainable advantage at the international level in the white goods industry.

In the four years after the acquisition, Electrolux turned Zanussi's 120 billion lire loss into 60 billion lire profit. Strategically more important, however, was the contribution Zanussi made to the restructuring of Electrolux's manufacturing, sales and component supply. By 1988 Electrolux faced different and sophisticated development needs. It needed to develop not just scale efficiencies, but also the organisational capabilities to keep adapting to local market needs. In other words it needed to develop co-ordination skills. Strategic industry issues reflect the organisational issues. Appliances usually need to combine national product features with regional and global manufacturing and research efficiencies. National strategies are successful in this industry, but the industry does appear to be moving from a national to a more global structure.

Changes occurring in the industry include supply-side changes: new types of production technology which make possible smaller efficient batch sizes and therefore changed production economies of scale; changes in component design which enable standard components to be used in many different models; international sourcing; changed transportation infrastructure leading to changed distribution and logistics for the industry. Any combination of these factors leads to fundamental shifts in the economics of the industry. Once this has happened, and once any single competitor has started to review their own strategy in order to benefit from the changed economics, different strategies will be visible in the industry. Inevitably those firms which are able to capture potential savings earliest will be in a stronger position, at least until others have caught up.

The other type of industry changes are changes in markets and may be described as demand-side changes (for example, new styles of consumer preferences which lead to shifts in patterns of demand). These may be as a result of media advertising or common foreign travel experiences which create greater similarity in acceptability of designs or product features across previously diverse markets. If this happens it accelerates the possibility of benefiting from the supply-side developments described above. A combination of these supply and demand characteristics affects the viability of historically successful strategies in an industry. It may make strategies which were previously considered inappropriate for the industry – regional or global strategies for white goods – become viable under the changed industry conditions.

Electrolux used the Zanussi acquisition to change its strategic positioning within the white goods industry worldwide. Historically in the white goods industry, competitive strategies had been based on domestic markets. Regional (e.g. pan-European) strategies were perceived as being inappropriate, high-risk and unprofitable. This widely held industry recipe was supported by research on the distinct nature of the various European markets and the competitive advantage accruing to national producers, with relative disadvantage to regional producers. These views were even more pronounced for global strategies (Baden-Fuller and Stopford, 1991). Local domestic manufacturers such as UK-based Hotpoint (with a pure UK domestic market strategy) were indeed more profitable than the regional, and soon-to-be global, strategy of Electrolux, at least for the time being. However, if these factors were well-understood and part of the shared knowledge-base in the white goods industry, why were companies like the US firm Whirlpool and the Swedish firm Electrolux starting to put in place the building blocks for a global strategy in white goods?

During the 1980s continued concentration (consolidation) occurred among companies competing in the European and global market-places for white goods. After Electrolux acquired Zanussi, the other world player in white goods, Whirlpool, acquired 53 per cent of the white goods business of the Dutch consumer electronics firm Philips in 1988, as discussed in Section 4.1.4.

We must be clear about the purpose of the Electrolux acquisition of Zanussi. The purpose of the acquisition was not to turn Zanussi around. That was simply the means to a larger end. The main purpose of the acquisition was to better enable Electrolux to implement its global strategy. How was this to be achieved? Through utilising Zanussi's assets in:

- complementary geographic markets to those of Electrolux
- complementary product categories to those of Electrolux
- technological innovation in R&D
- integration and rationalisation of production plants across Europe
- integration and rationalisation of sales and marketing across Europe
- worldwide integration of component design and production.

You may now appreciate the immensity of the task faced by Electrolux and the complexity and criticality of the organisational implementation issues. We may classify these as issues of configuration and co-ordination (as discussed in Section 3.3). Where should Electrolux locate its various business activities nationally, regionally or globally (i.e. organisational configuration) and how should it integrate them internationally for greatest efficiency and effectiveness (i.e. managerial co-ordination)? Put another way what we are discussing is the simple issue of how to construct an international value chain. That is the international value chain 'configuration' issue we discussed in Section 2.3. Following immediately from that is the value chain 'co-ordination' issue: having decided to integrate component production worldwide to benefit from design and production economies, how does Electrolux co-ordinate its information-gathering worldwide to ensure that these efficiently produced components are distributed when and where they are needed to their various production plants around the world?

Thus the organisational issues raised by the ability of Electrolux to integrate Zanussi are synonymous with the ability of Electrolux to implement the co-ordination required by its global strategy.

Reflection

At the end of this book, you may find it useful to reflect on your own job and consider how you personally are affected, either at work or in your personal life, by the issues raised here.

6 Summary and conclusion

In this book we have been extending the concepts and frameworks of strategic management to international strategy. In particular, we have emphasised the difference between the comparative advantage of nations and the competitive advantage of firms. Some managers, however, may feel this has little relevance to their jobs or their day-to-day responsibilities. We have tried throughout to convey the relevance, to individuals and to organisations, of issues faced in the international arena. The world's multinational corporations are the custodians of much wealth and potential power. Directly or indirectly, the decisions they make affect our daily lives. This book has attempted to explain why and how that is so, and what we can do to improve our own organisation's management practice.

Being a good global or local manager means understanding the business, and the competitive and macro-environmental contextual forces that impact on our ability to run our organisations. Organisations participating in the international strategy arena experience benefits: from exposure to the world's most demanding customers; in learning how to simultaneously meet global, regional and domestic market needs; in being better able to anticipate the moves of competitors or rivals (or even partners); in access to world-class technology; and in the transfer of best practice.

The emphasis in international strategy has been changing from a focus on global scale, factor costs, sourcing platforms and product standardisation, to a focus on customer needs, risk avoidance, variety at low cost and regional autonomy. This may be understood as a shift in emphasis from concern with the integration of international operations to a concern with strategic co-ordination and local responsiveness.

The pursuit of international advantage affects every nation, every organisation and every individual. The essence of international strategy is the exercise of a greater variety of options and opportunities arising from the existence of different skills and resources in different national markets. How organisations and governments interact in their attempts to control or capture those opportunities creates and defines the dynamics of international competition. The outcomes of these resource battles affect the daily lives of us all.

REFERENCES

Baden-Fuller, C.W. and Stopford, J.M. (1991) 'Globalisation frustrated: the case of white goods', *Strategic Management Journal*, Vol. 12, pp. 493–507.

Barney, J.B. (1996) *Gaining and Sustaining Competitive Advantage*, Addison-Wesley, Reading, MA.

Bartlett, C.A. (1986) 'Building and managing the transnational: the new organisational challenge' in Porter M. (ed.) *Competition in Global Industries*, Harvard Business School Press, Boston, MA.

Bartlett, C. and Ghoshal, S. (1986) 'Tap your subsidiaries for global reach', *Harvard Business Review*, November/December, pp. 87–94.

Bartlett, C. and Ghoshal, S. (1987) 'Managing across borders: new strategic requirements', *Sloan Management Review*, Summer, pp. 7–17.

Bartlett C. and Ghoshal, S. (1989) *Managing Across Borders: the transnational solution*, Hutchinson, London.

Bartlett, C. and Ghoshal, S. (1993) 'Beyond the M-form: towards a managerial theory of the firm', *Strategic Management Journal*, Vol. 14, pp. 23–46 (in Course Reader).

Carlzon, J. (1987) *Moments of Truth*, Ballinger Publishing Co., Cambridge, MA.

Chandler, A.D. (1962) *Strategy and Structure*, The MIT Press, Cambridge, MA.

Chandler, A.D. (1990) 'The enduring logic of industrial success', *Harvard Business Review*, March/April, pp. 130–40.

Christopher, M. and Braithwaite, A. (1994) 'Managing the global pipeline', in Segal-Horn, S. (ed.) *The Challenge of International Business*, Kogan Page, London.

De la Torre, J. and Neckar, D.H (1988) 'Forecasting political risks for international operations', *International Journal of Forecasting*, Vol. 4, pp. 221–41.

Douglas, S.P. and Wind, Y. (1987) 'The myth of globalization', *Columbia Journal of World Business*, Winter, pp. 19–29.

Faulkner, D.O. (1994) *International Strategic Alliances: co-operating to compete*, McGraw-Hill, Maidenhead.

Ghoshal, S. (1987) 'Global strategy: an organising framework', *Strategic Management Journal*, Vol. 8, pp. 425–40.

Hamel, G. (1991) 'Competition for competence and interpartner learning within international strategic alliances', *Strategic Management Journal*, Vol. 12, pp. 83–103.

Hamel, G. and Prahalad, C.K. (1985) 'Do you really have a global strategy?', *Harvard Business Review*, July/August, pp. 139–48.

Hamel, G. and Prahalad, C.K. (1989) 'Strategic intent', *Harvard Business Review*, May/June, pp. 63–76.

Hamel, G., Doz, Y.L. and Prahalad, C.K. (1989) 'Collaborate with your competitors – and win', *Harvard Business Review*, January/February, pp. 133–9.

Harrigan, K. (1984) 'Joint ventures and global strategies', *Columbia Journal of World Business*, Summer, pp. 7–16.

Hennart, J.F. (1988) 'A transaction cost theory of equity joint ventures', *Strategic Management Journal*, Vol. 9, pp. 361–74.

Kanter, R.M. (1988) 'When a thousand flowers bloom: structural, collective and social conditions for innovation in organisations', *Research in Organisational Behaviour*, Vol. 10, pp. 169–211.

Kay, J. (1993) *Foundations of Corporate Success*, Oxford University Press, Oxford.

Killing, P.J. (1992) 'How to make a global joint venture work', *Harvard Business Review*, May/June, pp. 120–7.

Kogut, B. (1985) 'Designing global strategies: profiting from operational flexibility', *Sloan Management Review*, Fall, pp. 27–38.

Levitt, T. (1983) 'The globalization of markets', *Harvard Business Review*, May/June, pp. 92–102.

Mohr, J. and Spekman, R. (1994) 'The characteristics of partnership success' *Strategic Management Journal*, Vol. 15, pp. 135–52.

Normann, R. (1984) *Service Management: strategy and leadership in service businesses*, Wiley, Chichester.

Ohmae, K. (1985) *Triad Power: the coming shape of global competition*, The Free Press, New York.

Ohmae, K. (1989) 'Managing in a borderless world', *Harvard Business Review*, May/June, pp. 152–61.

Porter, M.E. (1980) *Competitive Strategy*, The Free Press, New York.

Porter, M.E. (1986) *Competitiveness in Global Industries*, Harvard Business School Press, Boston, MA.

Porter, M.E. (1987) 'From competitive advantage to corporate strategy', *Harvard Business Review*, May/June, pp. 43–59.

Porter, M.E. (1990) *The Competitive Advantage of Nations*, Macmillan, Basingstoke.

Powell, W.W. (1990) 'Neither market nor hierarchy: network forms of organisation', *Research in Organisational Behaviour*, Vol. 12, pp. 295–336.

Prahalad, C.K. and Doz, Y. (1987) *The Multinational Mission*, The Free Press, New York.

Quelch, J.A. and Hoff, E.J. (1986) 'Customizing global marketing', *Harvard Business Review*, May/June, pp. 59–68.

Rugman, A.M., Lecraw, D.J. and Booth, L.D. (1985) *International Business: firm and environment*, McGraw-Hill, New York.

Sasser, W.E., Wycoff, D.D. and Olsen, M. (1978) *The Management of Service Operations*, Allyn and Bacon, London.

Segal-Horn, S. (1993) 'The internationalisation of service firms', *Advances in Strategic Management*, Vol. 9, pp. 31–55 (in Course Reader).

Whittington, R. (1993) *What is Strategy – and Does It Matter?*, Routledge, London.

Yip, G.S.(1989) 'Global strategy... in a world of nations?', *Sloan Management Review*, Fall, pp. 29–41.

Yip, G.S. (1992) *Total Global Strategy*, Prentice Hall, Englewood Cliffs, NJ.

Acknowledgements

Grateful acknowledgement is made to the following sources for permission to reproduce material in this book:

Text

Box 3.1: Porter v. Ohmae, *The Economist,* 4 August 1990, © 1990 Economist Newspapers Limited; *Box 3.2*: Gillette snaps up Duracell, *The Sunday Times,* 15 September 1996, © Times Newspapers Limited; *Box 4.1*: The discreet charm of the multicultural multinational, *The Economist,* 30 July 1994, © 1994 Economist Newspapers Limited.

Figures

Figure 2.3: Reprinted from *International Journal of Forecasting,* 4(2), Armstrong, J.S. Forecasting political risks for international operations, p.223, Copyright © 1988 with kind permission from Elsevier Science NL Sara Burgerhartstraat 25, 1055 KV Amsterdam, The Netherlands; *Figure 3.1*: Porter, M. 1990, *The Competitive Advantage of Nations,* p.342, Macmillan Press Limited; Figure 3.2: Reprinted by permission of Harvard Business School Press. From Competition in Global Industries by Porter, M., Boston, MA 1986. Copyright © 1986 by the President and Fellows of Harvard.

Tables

Table 2.1: Reprinted by permission of Harvard Business School Press and Century Hutchinson Limited. From *Competition in Global Industries* by Bartlett, C.A. and Ghoshal, S., Boston, MA 1989. Copyright © 1989 by the President and Fellows of Harvard; *Table 3.1*: Ghoshal, S. 1987, Global strategy: an organizing framework, *Strategic Management Journal,* **8**, © 1987 John Wiley and Sons Ltd, by permission of John Wiley and Sons Limited.

Photographs

Page 33: Henry Kravis, Rex Features Ltd; *Page 37*: Japan Information and Cultural Centre, Embassy of Japan.

BOOK 12

THE DYNAMICS OF STRATEGY

Authors: Susan Segal-Horn and Eric Cassells

MBA Strategy

Contents

1 **Introduction** — 5
 1.1 Learning objectives of this book — 5

2 **Why strategy matters** — 7
 2.1 Strategic learning makes a difference — 10
 2.2 Strategic learning and organisational structure — 12

3 **Strategy and the search for advantage** — 13
 3.1 Strategy and innovation — 14
 3.2 New ways to compete — 19
 3.3 Strategic positioning and operational effectiveness — 20
 3.4 Market positioning or resource leveraging — 22
 3.5 Summary — 26

4 **Sustainability** — 27
 4.1 Strategy and commitment — 31

5 **Summary and conclusion** — 32

References — 34

Acknowledgements — 35

1 Introduction

And the end of all our exploring
Will be to arrive where we started
And know the place for the first time.

(T.S. Eliot, 'Little Gidding', Collected Poems 1909–1962, Faber 1974, p. 222)

In the Introduction to Book 1, the prime purpose of the course was stated to be 'the improvement of the quality of your strategic thinking'. We asserted that mere knowledge of the models, frameworks and techniques of strategic analysis is a necessary, but not a sufficient, condition for effective strategic decision-making. Most managers in most types of organisation these days are in a position to read and learn about strategy and strategic ideas and models. That knowledge in itself is neither unique nor distinctive and it is certainly imitable. Far more important is your ability to use the models creatively and with confidence in the changing external and internal organisational contexts in which you have to manage. The idea that today all these contexts are 'turbulent' is almost a truism. Very few situations in which we have to function as managers are likely to be stable and predictable for more than relatively short periods of time. Your insight and imagination in applying the concepts you have learnt will help you handle these uncertainties. Strategy includes coping with uncertainty and with complexity and having to make important decisions with inadequate information – decisions which will affect the lives of many people other than yourself.

In this final book, we are concerned about your overall perspective on the subject of strategy and to reinforce a particular view of what has been most important in this course. You may find the style of this concluding book rather different from all the earlier ones. In this book we are not attempting to present many different approaches to issues and cases: we have done that in the preceding books. This final book is deliberately more directive. The intention is to provide as clear a statement as possible of what we mean by a strategic perspective.

We have asserted throughout this course that strategic management based on innovative strategic thinking does 'make a difference'. We shall revisit the subject of strategy, discussing why it is so important in management practice and how it makes that difference. During this final journey we shall seek out some places of special interest along the way – those places that show how best to use strategy and how to implement it. We wish to emphasise the practical importance of thinking strategically. The subject of strategy has a very practical purpose: strategy is ultimately about survival and, further, about helping organisations to flourish.

1.1 Learning objectives of this book

The overall learning objective of this book is to consolidate the previous learning from throughout the course. After studying this book you should be able to:

- explain why strategy matters for organisations

- understand what is meant by a strategic issue and strategic thinking
- demonstrate that strategy is about exercising judgement in whatever context, simple or complex
- demonstrate that strategy is integrative, holistic and iterative
- develop an overview of the scope and content of the subject of strategy, an ability to work with many of its frameworks and apply them, when appropriate, to managerial decision-making
- show that while the content of strategies will differ across sectors, the requirement for strategy does not.

2 Why strategy matters

The justification for studying strategy is that it makes a difference to the potential long-term survival of organisations.

Activity 2.1

You should now read the final worked case in the course, which focuses on Airbus in late 1996, and the intense competitive rivalry in the civil aircraft manufacturing industry. This worked case builds on the earlier mini-case on Airbus in Book 2.

Discussion

There are a number of worked case questions in the reading which require the reader to make judgements about truly strategic issues facing Airbus. Reflecting how far you have come in this course, these questions address great uncertainties for Airbus, dealing with problems which might be considered intractable. Nevertheless, strategists in this industry must make choices involving the long-term commitment of huge resources. The uncertainties in the industry are not of the same type as those depicted in the 'Information Superhighway' video you viewed earlier in the course. In that industry there were massive uncertainties about the very nature of the products and services needed, the configuration of competitors or competitive alliances, and the basis for competition. Unusually, the highly stylised nature of competition in the aircraft industry even allows us to model strategic choices and outcomes using game theory; something which would be practically impossible in the ICT sector. Instead, the uncertainties for Airbus concern the size of demand for the superjumbo product, the commercial and political constraints of restructuring, and – most crucially – just how Boeing will react to any single competitive move Airbus may make. This 'conjectural uncertainty' over how competitors might behave is at the very heart of strategic decision-making. Analysis of the situation, as the worked case shows, can only take strategists so far. Eventually, uncertain choices must be made.

The importance of these choices is also demonstrated by the Airbus case. Without the collaboration of European governments and national aircraft manufacturers over the preceding 25 years, the European industry would practically have ceased to exist, jobs and technological skills lost, independent defence capabilities undermined, Boeing's near-monopoly in certain product categories extended, and the bargaining power of airlines reduced. Airbus had, instead, built a coherent market position as the main (now sole) competitor to Boeing in the world aircraft industry. The choices facing Airbus in 1996 might also determine whether it finally ceded dominance of the industry to Boeing, whether it managed to out-compete Boeing, or collapsed under the enormous financial strain of developing the uncertain superjumbo project.

As is shown by the Airbus worked case, strategy 'makes a difference':

> Strategic management as a field of inquiry is firmly grounded in practice and exists because of the importance of its subject. The strategic direction of business organizations is at the heart of wealth creation in modern industrial society. The field has not, like political science, grown from ancient roots in philosophy, nor does it, like parts of economics, attract scholars because of the elegance of its theoretical underpinnings. Rather, like medicine or engineering, it exists because it is worthwhile to codify, teach, and expand what is known about the skilled performance of roles and tasks that are a necessary part of our civilization.
>
> (Rumelt et al., 1994, pp. 9–10)

In other words, the subject of strategy has developed because *practitioners* needed it. We learn about the theory of strategy because of its *practical* importance to all types of organisation. The practice of strategy is concerned with identifying issues that 'make a difference'.

Activity 2.2

Consider the Jollibee mini-case which follows. Think carefully about its strategy.

What enabled it to beat McDonald's in the Philippines?

Did Jollibee succeed for strategic or mainly for operational reasons?

MINI-CASE: JOLLIBEE

'I suppose we've done nothing but beat McDonald's at their own game.'

(Menlou B. Bibonia, VP Marketing, Jollibee; quoted in *Business Week*, 1 July 1996)

For Jollibee Foods Corporation, beating McDonald's meant gaining a 46 per cent share of the fast food market in the Philippines by 1995, compared with McDonald's 16 per cent share. This was achieved from equal market shares of about 20 per cent in the mid-1980s.

Jollibee's offering

Some of Jollibee's success has come from a little luck and some from the imitation of McDonald's fast food technology: Jollibee's approach claims similar standards of cleanliness and fast service, and copies McDonald's overall marketing methods and emphasis on convenient and popular locations. The luck arose when Jollibee benefited in the mid-1980s from McDonald's limited expansion in the Philippines during a time of political instability.

Jollibee has, however, brought something unique to the Filipino fast food market. Instead of copying McDonald's menu, Jollibee commissioned research to identify the preferences of the average Filipino. As a result, Jollibee's menu offers a distinctive sweet and sour sauce along with its burgers, fried chicken, and spaghetti. These main dishes are served with rice rather than fries. Jollibee's burger is commonly agreed to be juicer, spicier, and sweeter than the typical McDonald's patty and is similar to what a typical Filipina mother might cook. Jollibee's distinctive menu has been offered at 5 or 10 per cent less than the comparable McDonald's offering.

The success of Jollibee is perhaps best recognised by McDonald's decision in 1995 to launch their own fried chicken, rice, spaghetti, and sweet and spicy burger (the 'McDo') menu in the Philippines. It was believed that the Philippines was the only country in the world where McDonald's had allowed the flavour of their traditional hamburger to be changed.

Promoting Jollibee

Jollibee's marketing, although based on McDonald's approach, is widely credited as being more successful. Characters such as 'Jollibee' (a yellow-and-orange bumblebee), 'Hetty' (a blonde spaghetti-haired girl), and 'Champ' (a burger-headed boxer), appear to appeal to Filipino children more than McDonald's own 'Ronald McDonald'. These characters are promoted through heavy advertising to appeal to the Filipino family's tradition of treating children at weekends.

Similarly, Jollibee places the same emphasis on acquiring the right locations for outlets as McDonald's traditionally has. The key objective of their expansion strategy is to be the first fast food restaurant in key locations such as new shopping malls. Where this objective is not met, Jollibee responds aggressively to McDonald's through a strategy of 'clustering' outlets. Thus, McDonald's outlet in Manila's Megamall is surrounded by three Jollibee restaurants. This means that a customer must pass a Jollibee outlet before they can arrive at a McDonald's. On a typical weekend day, all three Jollibee outlets in the Megamall are busier than the sole McDonald's. By 1995, there were 177 Jollibee restaurants in the Philippines, compared with 90 McDonald's. Thirty-six new outlets were planned for 1996.

International expansion

The aggressive domestic expansion of the Jollibee chain is equalled by an ambition to open 500 overseas outlets by the year 2000. This compares with a total of over 2,600 McDonald's outlets in Asia alone in 1995. Appealing initially to large Filipino expatriate communities in the Middle East and Southeast Asia, Jollibee had opened 15 outlets by 1995, with another 20 planned in 1996. Jollibee has, however, partially adapted its menu to local tastes in the countries it has opened in. It also deliberately targets markets where McDonald's are weaker, or which they have overlooked. Thus, there are five Jollibee outlets in Brunei, where McDonald's have only one restaurant. 1996 will also mark the opening of two Jollibee restaurants in McDonald's US heartland, appealing initially to the Filipino immigrants of San Francisco and Los Angeles.

(Adapted from Business Week, *1 July 1996)*

Discussion

Jollibee's success in beating McDonald's in the Philippines demonstrates clearly that strategy, and the choices managers make about strategy, matter.

McDonald's is one of the great business success stories of the last forty years. It has expanded to become the world's largest global restaurant chain. Despite being much imitated, McDonald's has generally retained its pre-eminent position and continued to expand successfully around the world.

Jollibee's market share success against McDonald's seems to stem from three main strategy processes:

1. *Successfully imitating McDonald's operational systems and procedures for fast food delivery, as well as its product concept of a limited, burger-based menu.*

> 2   *Redefining the broad product concept to develop a distinctive local product offering, carefully targeted at local tastes. This offers a clear contrast to McDonald's 'international' menu based on the traditional American burger.*
>
> 3   *Outperforming McDonald's in the constant battle for prime locations and successful marketing campaigns.*

Jollibee's strategy was aggressive and ambitious. Not only was it willing to incur the cost of opening additional 'cluster' outlets to surround prime McDonald's outlets in the Philippines, but in addition, Jollibee's international expansion has been undeniably ambitious. To use some of the vocabulary from Book 11, Jollibee is attacking McDonald's global strategy (based on global standardisation) by providing a contrasting product adapted for the Philippines domestic market. This pushed McDonald's into providing an adapted product (the 'McDo') especially for the Filipino market, to counterattack Jollibee's success. In its international expansion Jollibee has picked off markets to which McDonald's has been indifferent, and is now entering its competitor's home market. It is one thing to take on an organisation as apparently dominant as McDonald's in Jollibee's home territories, but to target their entrenched international and domestic market position is brave indeed. In pursuing this international strategy, Jollibee is building its growth ambitions initially on the unique resource of appeal to widespread Filipino emigrant communities, and on the weaknesses they perceive in McDonald's international strategy in countries where they are poorly represented. Jollibee's international growth strategy relies heavily on its ambition to stretch its resources, in a way reminiscent of Komatsu's vision of 'encircling' Caterpillar in the global earth-moving equipment industry (see the mini-case in Book 11). At the beginning of their attack in the 1960s Caterpillar, too, was considered unassailable both globally and in their US domestic market, and Komatsu was not taken seriously as a potential rival.

Efficient operations to match those of McDonald's were a necessary (but not sufficient) condition for Jollibee's success; it was their clarity of strategic direction and distinctive market positioning which were critical to seeing and targeting the potential gap in the market. A direct attack on a much stronger competitor would not have been effective for Jollibee. However, it is interesting to note that at an earlier stage it would have been easy for McDonald's to have adapted their offering slightly (as Kentucky Fried Chicken did in Japan) to close the window of opportunity that they left for Jollibee to identify and exploit.

2.1   STRATEGIC LEARNING MAKES A DIFFERENCE

The important lesson to take from the Jollibee mini-case, as well as from many of the earlier cases in the course, is that strategic analysis and strategic thinking make a difference to the potential opportunities available to an organisation. Choices about strategy can make a difference to the survival and prosperity of an organisation, even when the competitive hurdles facing it are extremely high. Beyond the initial stages of selecting a viable strategy and implementing it effectively is a further, more sophisticated, stage for any organisation which we have referred to many times during the course: 'learning how to learn'. The practice of strategic learning, therefore, must be concerned primarily with learning how to continuously identify and deal with strategic issues as they emerge, since there are many kinds of strategic issue. What is genuinely of strategic importance will change over time with organisational, industry, or market change – or all three.

In the course video, 'A New Way of Life', BP's Atlantic Frontier Programme asset manager, Colin MacLean, argued that the development of large-scale strategic assets such as oil fields required its own kind of learning. Unlike the learning that occurs from the repetition of standardised operations (which can be a source of advantage where experience-curve benefits are relevant), learning on these development projects, where each one has unique features, is specifically concerned with developing a capability to make decisions about strategic issues:

> Let's consider that every new discovery is a little cloud of problems. You may think that discovering an oil field is a moment of celebration, the work is finished, and BP has made another excellent discovery. How it shows up for the teams of people working on the discovery, however, is as a little cloud of problems. How are we going to solve these things? How are we going to take this discovery and move it through to the point where we produce barrels of oil? Now there are two ways to deal with this little pile of problems called the discovery. ...

> By working every problem to death, I mean writing learned reports on every problem, be they small or big problems – putting them together in beautifully prepared reports, getting people like me, the manager, to sign off, saying, 'This is a very important piece of work'. ... Inevitably those things end up in files or libraries. ... The investment decision is taken, the project is developed, the field goes on production and it doesn't behave the way people expect it to behave. We then get the post-project audit report – the famous post-project audit – in which people write down why it didn't work, and that in turn is filed, and we never learn. Libraries are full of this type of learning; we as humans are empty of it. ...

> There is an alternative though. Let's take the same problems, the same little clouds of concern. ... Let's look into that cloud with teams who are trained to look at what's going to make a difference here. Not everything is going to make a difference. ... So we distinguish those problems that are going to make a difference if intervened against: which are going to make the project highly profitable, and which problems, if we do nothing about them, are going to kill us. We get a very small sub-set of that big cloud of concern which used to be the discovery, a little sub-set of those problems that are going to make a difference. Then we go to work on these problems – not understanding them for their own sake, not writing learned reports about them, but actually inventing interventions to put in place should those problems come about.

(Source: OUBS recorded interview material)

Strategic learning is what is needed and what will be used, not filed and left unused. Strategic learning is what leads to action. It is a competitive capability, one that can lead to competitive advantage. As Colin MacLean says:

> It's not just the learning – it's not just being able to sit back after the action and say: 'I learnt the following, and I will write a recipe book so that someone else doesn't make the same mistake or that someone else can do it.' ... It's the pace at which you learn which matters. ... Lessons are learnt daily and they're put into action immediately. So it's the pace of learning on Foinaven [a North Atlantic oilfield] which enhances our company's performance and the next projects we do. ...

> It's fundamental to our success as a business that we create the industry in a way which will provide more profitable outcomes. The key to this is continual ongoing education and support of people so they can take on bigger risks and understand the consequences of taking these risks.
>
> (Source: OUBS recorded interview material)

2.2 STRATEGIC LEARNING AND ORGANISATIONAL STRUCTURE

Strategic learning as a distinctive capability is achieved, therefore, through the explicit realisation that strategic recipes will not work in dealing with novel strategic issues, that learning to manage uncertainty involves learning to manage and take risks, and that competing across time involves learning to learn more quickly. The organisational structure frameworks that you were introduced to in Books 8 and 11, such as the M-form (multidivisional) and the N-form (network) organisations, were all attempting to deal with the same issue: how to continually develop organisational structures that are more effective at letting the people within them adapt, innovate and learn from each other to cope with complex environments. This tends to be less of a problem in smaller organisations where contact is more informal, frequent and face-to-face. In all large organisations, or in co-operative alliances across large organisations, the attainment of such organisational flexibility and adaptability to enable the transfer of learning is one of the most intransigent managerial problems. Providing an organisational structure in which learning can take place (or at least not be unduly inhibited) is an important organisational capability in itself.

3 Strategy and the Search for Advantage

The search for advantage is at the heart of the practice of strategy. This is because all organisations depend for their survival on acquiring scarce resources, whether financial, intellectual, managerial, technological, structural or human, and making an adequate return on them to satisfy their stakeholders. To the extent that this is true, competition to acquire resources and to use them most effectively is at the heart of strategy. For most organisations, moreover, a superior return on all such resources is more desirable than simply an adequate one. The key to achieving those superior returns is through identifying distinctive resources and capabilities and then building upon them to provide current and future sources of advantage.

Activity 3.1

Please read the mini-case on Aprilia motorcycles.

What sources of potential advantage does it identify on which to build its competitive strategy?

MINI-CASE: APRILIA MOTORCYCLES

Ivano Beggio's company Aprilia has quadrupled sales from just over $100 million in 1992 to nearly $500 million in 1996. How, then, does an Italian motorcycle manufacturer succeed in an industry dominated by large Japanese manufacturers such as Honda and Yamaha, and established US companies such as Harley Davidson? By being different, apparently.

Whereas Harley Davidson sells an image of a hard-driving, hard-living male lifestyle, and Honda and Yamaha rely on their reputations for build quality and engineering excellence, Aprilia has chosen to sell motorbikes that are distinctively European. Aprilia has a range of 18 motorcycles and scooters, which emphasise European design motifs and signatures. Their best-selling 650 cc 'Moto', for example, has been designed by French designer Philippe Starck, drawing on the same post-modern styling he uses for his buildings and furniture.

In addition, Aprilia builds its bikes in co-operation with a network of 150 component manufacturers in Northern Italy. Aprilia undertakes the design, final assembly and marketing of its bikes, but does not manufacture a single component itself. This approach has enabled it to access the most advanced technology that suppliers can offer. It is also believed to reduce cost and promote manufacturing flexibility; Aprilia's operating margins of 10 per cent are twice the average in the industry.

Although its sales are derived primarily from the European market, in 1996 Aprilia was on the verge of launching ventures in China (the fastest-growing motorcycle market in the world), and the US (where the bikes already have a strong cult following through import sales).

(Adapted from Business Week, *10 June 1996)*

Discussion _____

As you may remember from the Honda case discussed in Book 9, the motorcycle industry is extremely competitive, with very high levels of rivalry between entrenched market leaders pursuing different competitive strategies based on image, power, product range, technical capabilities, and so on. Nevertheless, we know that strategies with something distinctive to offer can succeed. Here we may use the Porter 'diamond' (see Book 11, Section 3.2) to demonstrate that Aprilia used some distinctive sources of advantage rooted in its national 'cluster': a large and discerning Italian home market; Italian style and design skills; inviting the innovative ideas of a French modern furniture designer; low-cost, decentralised network manufacturing. Together these made possible a new type of 'post-modern designer' bike which provided the basis for a profitable and growing niche.

3.1 STRATEGY AND INNOVATION

Aprilia motorcycles has been successful within a mature industry, confirming Baden-Fuller and Stopford's arguments for 'rejuvenation' in their article in the Course Reader. There may indeed be no such things as mature products or mature markets, only tired strategies, an over-reliance on industry recipes (Book 1) and a lack of innovative strategic thinking by managers. Aprilia's growth and superior operating margins were attributable to product innovation based on distinctive styling emphasising European design, together with a network manufacturing operation. Consider the examples from the airline industry in the mini-case below.

MINI-CASE: INNOVATING TO COMPETE – AIRLINE INNOVATION 1

Líneas Aéreas Privadas Argentinas (LAPA)

Gustavo Deutsch acquired a ranch, two propeller aircraft and an airline in 1984. Deutsch held on to the airline because of the prospect of deregulation of the airline industry in Argentina. Deregulation of domestic scheduled routes did not, in fact, occur until 1994, when LAPA started flying jets in direct competition to Aerolíneas Argentinas, and its domestic carrier, Austral.

Like other airlines such as SouthWest in the USA, Ryanair in Ireland, and AeroRepublica in Colombia, LAPA offered cut-rate fares on point-to-point domestic routes. Between Buenos Aires and Córdoba, for example, LAPA's standard single $59 fare undercut the $148 and $168 fares of Aerolíneas and Austral, respectively. To enable these low fares, LAPA limited its service: refreshments were limited to soft drinks, coffee and champagne; with no meals to serve, galleys could be stripped out and extra seats installed; fewer cabin crew were needed; no meals meant less loading, so airport turnaround times could be reduced. Overheads were also controlled through outsourcing, with reservations being handled by American Airlines, aircraft maintenance by LANChile, and a frequent-flyer programme by United Airlines.

> LAPA's strategy was remarkably successful, increasing its domestic market share from 1.2 per cent in 1992 to 20 per cent (1.2 million passengers) in 1996. Revenues amounted to $100 million in 1996, and the fleet included eight Boeing jets and two Saab turboprops, and three Boeing 737s on order. Standardising the jet fleet on Boeings reduced the cost of maintenance.
>
> The low-price fare strategy was also helping to expand the market for air travel in Argentina, where total domestic passengers were expected to increase from 5 million in 1996 to 10 million in 2000. In addition, further deregulation allowed LAPA to start flying to neighbouring Uruguay, Brazil and Chile in 1996, with the prospect of all international flights from Argentina being deregulated by 2000. LAPA had, however, stated its aim to dominate the domestic market by this date, and not to compete in the long-distance international market.
>
> (Adapted from Business Week, 10 June 1996)

Deregulation in the airline industry has produced many opportunities for innovative strategies by new entrants. A number of airlines like LAPA are operating no-frills services in various markets throughout the world, matching a low-cost structure to a low-price strategy. This provides an important alternative to full service for passengers travelling short- and medium-haul flights.

The competitive innovation of airlines like LAPA followed a period in the 1980s when airlines such as American Airlines, British Airways, and Scandinavian Airlines System pursued what was then an innovative strategy based on differentiated levels of customer service to attract more high-value business customers, and developed the hub-and-spoke network system for integrating their route structures. By 1990 this new strategy had become the new industry recipe, the accepted way to compete among the world's airlines.

These innovations, however, carried extra costs and required higher fares consistent with a high-cost, high-price, high-added-value strategy. This in effect also provided a price umbrella – an opportunity for prospective new entrants who could compete with low-cost, low-price, no-frills offerings. SouthWestern in the USA was the first of a new breed of limited-service, low-fare airlines to take advantage of this opportunity which arose wherever airline industry deregulation occurred. These new entrant airlines paid a great deal of attention to reducing costs. They deliberately avoided the high-fixed-cost structure of operating hub-and-spoke networks, choosing to fly point-to-point routes over short and medium distances where customers cared less about service levels, and where flexible staffing arrangements meant staff utilisation was maximised (for example, cabin staff usually also handled boarding arrangements).

However, a range of possible ways for organisations to compete and to grow exists in all sectors and industries, public or private, service or product. Distinctiveness can come from innovations of very different types even within the same industry. British Airways took a different route to innovation in the airline industry, and, although BA is considered to be very successful, it must still seek further, continuous sources of innovation.

Activity 3.2

Now read the airline innovation mini-case 2 on British Airways.

If it is the world's most profitable airline, why does it need a new strategy?

What does this tell you about the relationship between strategy and innovation?

MINI-CASE: INNOVATING TO COMPETE – AIRLINE INNOVATION 2

British Airways (BA)

British Airways in 1996 had the reputation of being the world's most profitable airline, in an industry bedevilled by low profitability or massive losses. The former state-owned airline had been privatised in 1987, following programmes to make it leaner and more efficient. It had also painstakingly built a reputation for high standards of customer service from a poor reputation pre-privatisation.

The industry context

Apart from the US domestic market, markets in 1996 were still regulated through civil authorities' control of route access and airport landing 'slots'. Considerable pressure for further deregulation existed. In Europe, the EU saw the lack of competition and high price of flying as inhibiting the growth of air travel, and hence of the European economy generally. Internationally, the US government was pressurising other countries to adopt an 'open skies' policy.

In Europe, national airlines (mostly nationalised) were generally regarded as relatively inefficient, and often supported by large government subsidies. International routes had traditionally been regulated through bilateral agreements allowing national suppliers to create duopolies on individual routes. BA faced international competition mainly from the US airlines (many of whom had already been through a decade of intense domestic competition), the relatively inefficient European national airlines, and the competitive Asian airlines (Singapore Airlines, for example, was widely regarded as highly efficient, strongly customer-orientated and relatively low-cost). BA's single most important asset, however, was its unique dominant position as the owner of a majority of the 'slots' at London Heathrow, the busiest hub airport in the world.

The threats to BA

However, BA's superior competitive position was threatened by a number of changes occurring or pending.

Competition on short- and medium-haul routes had been revolutionised by deregulation which had allowed low-cost, 'no frills' suppliers such as easyJet in the UK, Virgin Express in Belgium, and Ryanair in Ireland to underprice traditional full service airlines by up to 70 per cent.

The UK government was under considerable political and economic pressure to negotiate an 'open skies' treaty with the USA. The opening of European skies to US competitors threatened a more intense phase of competition. While this might not threaten BA's existence as it might less efficient European airlines, it would affect its profitability. Intense domestic market competition may have eroded the profits of the US airlines, but it had also taught American Airlines, Delta and United how to survive through efficiency.

The EU had finally passed legislation preventing the further use of state subsidy to support loss-making national airlines, such as Air France, Sabena, Iberia and Alitalia. However, the political price of this agreement had been to allow one last large round of subsidies running into billions of dollars to the less competitive national airlines.

The best of the European airlines had been trying to catch up with BA in the early 1990s, so competitive differences between KLM and Lufthansa, and BA were assumed to have dwindled. Loss-making airlines such as Air France and Alitalia also planned efficiency programmes.

All the above were likely to lead to increased future competition in BA's principal markets, price wars, and pressure on BA's revenues.

BA's strategy for staying in front

1. *Costs* – Robert Ayling had taken over as Executive Chairman of BA in January 1996 and in September 1996 he announced a programme to find a further $1.5 billion of annual savings by 1999, partially through seeking voluntary redundancies of 5,000 staff. At the same time, customer services and language skills were to be further emphasised in staff training.

2. *Global route network alliances* – BA's strategy also focused on its international route network and its unique position at Heathrow. First, in May 1996 BA and American Airlines – previously the most bitter among all the transatlantic rivals – announced an alliance of their two networks. This followed a costly earlier attempt to gain access to USAir's domestic network, through acquiring a substantial 25 per cent minority stake. As BA had no access to internal US markets, the alliance with American would create a unique integrated network of American's US domestic, Latin American and transatlantic networks, with BA's strong international network and control of Heathrow. This alliance was subject to regulatory approval, and BA and American's competitors were determined to fight the alliance.

3. *Feeder route networks* – In addition, BA had in the early 1990s acquired control over TAT and Deutsche BA airlines to provide channels to feed French and German domestic traffic on to BA's international flights. These actions had put increased pressure on Air France and Lufthansa in their home markets.

4. *Franchising* – BA's global network was not an effective counter to the threat from low-cost regional airlines. BA's successful efficiency strategy of the 1980s and early 1990s made it difficult to save money simply by cutting more costs on existing operations. A new low-cost way to operate had to be found. BA had therefore introduced a strategy of franchising many of its UK domestic flights to other operators, such as ManxAir and LoganAir. Franchisers paid BA a fee, and were required to fly in BA colours, with BA staff uniforms, under the brand, 'British Air Express'. In 1996, BA extended this policy of franchising to its less profitable international routes, with the granting of a franchise to British Mediterranean Airways to fly to Beirut, Amman and Damascus.

5. *Outsourcing* – Changes to the ownership of services delivered under the BA brand were not limited to franchising routes. By 1996, BA had set up an independent business to run its maintenance and overhaul services, and compete for business direct from other airlines. Ayling's strategy targeted cargo and baggage handling, catering and accounting as other areas which might well be outsourced. Domenico Cempella, CEO of

> Alitalia, feared BA were 'going to outsource everything but their core operations' (*Business Week*, 30 September 1996). This statement did not, however, identify just what an airline's core operations were. Some analysts believed that an airline's core strategic business was the management of the route networks, and traffic and reservations systems. All other activities could be outsourced – even flying aircraft.
>
> (Adapted from Business Week, *3 June 1996; 30 September 1996*)

Discussion

After experiencing a number of years as the pre-eminent competitor in the international airline industry, BA was faced with real threats to its continuing prosperity. On domestic and regional flights, price has become a critical dimension of competition. The new 'no-frills' airlines threatened BA from below. On global and international networks they were threatened by the improving efficiency of the best of their European competitors, the lower cost base and high service levels of the Asian international airlines and by the aggressive expansion since deregulation of the large, efficient US airlines. Ever greater utilisation is essential to maintain profitability from the global network in the face of this competition.

Threatened at both ends of its business, the airline therefore set about inventing a new way of operating, turning its back on its full-service approach in all markets. Instead, franchising the less profitable international and domestic routes allowed a BA-branded service to be offered by lower-cost operators in alliance with BA. The international threat was being addressed in three main ways:

1. *attacking European competitors in their home markets by siphoning off domestic customers feeding on to international flights*
2. *pursuing a grand alliance with American Airlines to create the world's first global network, benefiting from their respective strengths: American's prime position in the US domestic market, and BA's effective control of a major world hub*
3. *further efficiency gains to enhance their cost advantage over competitors to make the task of catching up even more challenging for the national European airlines.*

Outsourcing major (but not strategic) activities, combined with franchising, was at the innovative heart of these strategies.

It is often difficult for a major organisation with a strong sense of identity and history to question a strategic recipe that has served it well for a number of years, especially when measures of current performance still indicate ongoing success through relatively high levels of profitability. BA's approach to rethinking and revising core components of its strategy in 1996 indicates an unusual willingness to question its ability to sustain that level of success into the future, unless significant changes were made to the way it competed. This reinforces once again the dynamic, rather than static, nature and context of strategy.

The mini-cases on LAPA and BA indicate that innovations in strategy within an industry can come in many forms, from entrepreneurial new entrants or long-established competitors. LAPA's success came about through identifying the opportunity created by deregulation for new types of competitive strategies exploiting the weakness of subsidised and previously protected Aerolíneas Argentinas. Demand existed for a different type of service. British Airways, on the other hand, recognised that its brand name was a considerable asset (a potential economy of scope) available for use across a variety of services. It had to find the best ways to exploit this in different market segments, against different competitors. Its innovation lies in seeking efficiencies by focusing strictly on core activities, while relying on a variety of partners to deliver the other activities required to fly passengers around the world.

Both LAPA and BA represent distinctive styles of innovation, showing ways to overcome the problems and exploit the strategic opportunities that face them in their respective market-places. Each of them is also acting within, and reacting to, the successive iterations of the dominant logic within their own industry or any industry (see Bettis and Prahalad, 1995) – by which we mean the way that industry recipes dominate, stagnate, create opportunities for innovation and are then in turn replaced.

3.2 NEW WAYS TO COMPETE

Willingness to challenge the accepted strategic recipes that have found favour in the past comes not only from introducing radically different products such as Sony's Walkman portable audios but also from thinking 'outside the box' about how things are done in an industry or sector. That may involve substituting collaboration for confrontation with suppliers, such as occurred in the Andrew Alliance in the 'New Way of Life' course video, or in the network supply arrangements of Aprilia in the mini-case above. Innovation may involve collaborating with competitors in select areas, where the resources and capabilities of one or other of the collaborators are inadequate for a chosen strategy. In the emerging electronic multimedia industry, for instance, collaboration between media, telecommunications and information technology companies is necessary for access to the diverse capabilities required even to participate in the industry. In 1996, the UK telecommunications sector saw six direct competitors, including Mercury Communications, TeleWest, and Nynex CableComms, form a venture to combine their networks. This was a collaboration to compete against British Telecom. Meanwhile, British Telecom was simultaneously pursuing a merger of its international operations with MCI (now part of WorldCom), the second largest US long-distance operator, to allow more effective international competition against AT&T.

'Thinking the unthinkable' can apply to how existing products or services are delivered, which may generate original concepts in otherwise very traditional sectors, as in the following suggestions about carpets.

> We're also thinking about ... the total life-cycle of the things we produce. What happens after they leave us? How do they end up? People buy an awful lot of things, not because they want them, but because they want what they can do.
>
> Carpet is a close-to-home example for Monsanto, since we are a leading maker of carpet fibre. People really don't want to own carpet. They just want to walk on carpet in their homes. What would happen if the carpet manufacturer owned the carpet and promised to replace it when it

needed replacing? If we could get the old carpet back, we could afford to put more cost into it in the first place to make it more recyclable.

We're looking at all our products from the standpoint of managing their total life-cycle. We're asking, what is it that people really need to buy? Do they need the stuff, or do they need the service? And what would the economics of making it a service look like?

(Shapiro, 1996, p. 13)

3.3 STRATEGIC POSITIONING AND OPERATIONAL EFFECTIVENESS

In the previous section we were illustrating one of the main themes of the course: that strategy is not static but dynamic. It is not something to be done once and then fixed for the whole future of an organisation, or dusted off every three years at the beginning of a new planning cycle. Over the longer term, and sometimes in the short term, all sources of advantage must be reviewed. Processes of competition can erode and eliminate sources of competitive advantage. Indeed advantage can be very difficult to sustain over the long term as the cartoon in Figure 3.1 suggests.

Figure 3.1 'Phase One of our strategy – getting out of the frying pan – was an unqualified success.'

Distinctive market positioning rarely stands alone as a source of potential superior performance. As shown in the two airline mini-cases above, it must usually be combined with operational effectiveness in implementation. In order to emphasise the important relationship between the two, and to illustrate this relationship between strategy and operations as fundamental to effective strategic management, let us consider the example of the Red Cross charity. Like all organisations, the Red Cross exists in a competitive marketplace for the resources it needs to continue to function, even if it does not use the language of competition internally or externally to describe itself and its role.

Activity 3.3

Please read Box 3.1 on the changes facing the Red Cross.

What are the issues it faces in terms of its operational effectiveness?

For what reasons might these pressures for change have arisen?

Does this mean that the Red Cross strategy has also changed?

BOX 3.1 CHARITY GIVEN A FACELIFT

Upheaval, redundancy and the dreaded 'downsizing' have been familiar in the private sector throughout the nineties. But this has not just been in hard-nosed, profit-motivated companies. Many voluntary sector organisations have also been forced to cut staff levels.

The Red Cross is rarely off our TV screens – three Red Cross nurses murdered in cold blood in Chechnya; food parcels for asylum seekers in London; Red Cross officials the only people allowed into the siege at the Japanese embassy in Lima.

But despite its prominence, this organisation has itself been in need of medical attention. Mike Whitlam was headhunted five years ago from the Royal National Institute of the Deaf to become [UK] director of the Red Cross. He was in Angola this week with Princess Diana, pursuing the campaign to ban landmines, and has had to negotiate something of a minefield at home in restructuring the organisation.

He says that when he took over at the Red Cross it was bureaucratic, costly and inefficient. Each local branch operated independently. There was a lack of accountability, it was difficult to implement national policy and ensure adequate standards were met. Because there was no regional network there was a gulf between national guidelines and local implementation. 'The trustees felt that the Red Cross had lost its sense of direction and its priorities,' he says.

Change was needed, but first it was necessary to buy time. The first goal of a five-year strategic plan was to raise the charity's profile. 'This was a high-risk strategy,' Whitlam admits. 'But the charity was doing a lot of good work, for which it was not being recognised.'

Other goals were to increase income, to improve the quality of support staff, review the range of services provided, and to reconfirm its work as a volunteer organisation, launching a programme of recruitment and support for the 90,000 volunteers and 2,700 staff.

The review process lasted 18 months. 'People weren't used to thinking about change,' says Whitlam. 'Therefore the review process became part of the change process. it was a difficult time for the staff. They feared for their jobs.'

On October 16 last year, when the Council approved the report, the suspense ended and some of those fears were justified. Forty thousand letters were sent to all volunteers and staff. Whitlam and the chairman, Elspeth Thomas, cancelled all commitments for a week and did a series of roadshows across the country, explaining the changes to staff and volunteers.

There will be 70 redundancies, the charitable status of individual branches across the UK will be dissolved and the society will become one body on January 1, 1998. A single national trustee body will be created, there will be eight regional offices which will support the branches in delivering increased services to local people.

There will be one-off costs of £6 million, funding new IT systems and relocation costs; the eight new regional offices will be funded by savings from headquarters and the regions. Once implemented, there will be savings of £7.4 million, and by the year 2000 80p in the pound will go to services and 20p to admin.

What difficulties do they still face? 'Change is a very painful process. People have written tomes on change management. Our main job is to keep people,

> not to lose good staff who may be uncertain that they see the benefits and advantages of the changes. There is still a lot of work to do,' says Whitlam.
>
> (*Source:* The Guardian *18 January 1997*)

Discussion

It is stated in the article that the Red Cross had become 'bureaucratic, costly and inefficient', with a lack of accountability between local branches and head office. Accountability is a serious problem in the voluntary sector, since it is largely dependent on public donations for funding to support activities worldwide and must retain public (stakeholder) trust in how such donations are spent. Increased central control through the creation of one national trustee body and a formal regional structure to replace local autonomy, combined with investment in IT systems for more effective information and control systems, should considerably increase managerial efficiency and credibility. People do not give money to charities to feel that it is spent on administration rather than on helping people. Therefore, credibility ultimately rests on retaining public confidence that 'by the year 2000 80p in the pound [sterling] will go to services and 20p to administration'. That means that operational effectiveness is critical to enabling the Red Cross to sustain its strategy and purpose, as well as stakeholder confidence.

The Red Cross (like its associates, such as the Red Crescent) has one of the most distinguished and best respected names ('brands') in the world. It is recognised and trusted worldwide. Yet even an organisation which appears to have such a clear purpose can lose its sense of direction if its operational effectiveness is undermined. Implementation of a strategy is as important as the analysis which gave rise to that strategy. It must be supported by appropriate internal control systems to achieve its declared objectives. A charity must be *especially* responsible in giving the most value possible for the resources entrusted to it.

3.4 MARKET POSITIONING OR RESOURCE LEVERAGING

We will return now to a debate which was first discussed earlier in the course in Book 4, Section 1.2.1. There you were introduced to the resource-based view of strategy as the emergent strategy paradigm for the 1990s, displacing the market positioning view of strategy which had been dominant in the 1980s.

Activity 3.4

Please read Box 3.2 about the debate between Porter and Hamel on the future direction and purpose of strategy.

Why is *The Economist* article sceptical about Hamel's view of strategy as 'stretching a firm's skill' to take advantage of a future market?

BOX 3.2 MAKING STRATEGY

The debate about strategy is shifting from the abstract question of what it is to the more practical question of how you make it.

Having spent the last few years with their head under the bonnet, fine-tuning the engine, many business people are now turning to the bigger question of where the car is pointed. A recent survey by the Association of Management Consulting Firms found that businessmen, academics and consultants expect business strategy to be their most pressing management issue in the next five years.

Asking a management theorist to define strategy is rather like asking a philosopher to define truth. But strategy is basically about two things: deciding where you want your company to go, and then how you want to take it there. Back in the 1970s most firms still relied on an annual 'strategic plan' produced by a specialised department. This has not lasted. Delegating decisions about direction to people who belonged neither in the engine-room nor on the bridge was a bad way to generate new ideas in fast-changing industries.

Still, the disappearance of strategic-planning departments has not eliminated the need for strategy. A company is well advised to know where it is heading. And the search for strategy without strategic planning has taken firms in some rum directions (mission statements, 'visioning' and all that). That may be why last year saw a fusillade of articles trying to redefine what strategy means.

Michael Porter, a professor at Harvard Business School, argued that strategy was about finding the position in the market-place that best suits a firm's skills. But in an article that narrowly beat Mr Porter's to win the annual McKinsey award for the best article in the *Harvard Business Review*, Gary Hamel, a professor at London Business School, suggested that strategy meant deciding what a future market will look like and then stretching a firm's skills so that it could take advantage of that market.

Put that way, Mr Hamel's theory sounds a little, well, theoretical. Imagining future markets is all very well in Silicon Valley; but how on earth is one dog-food company's vision of the future going to differ from those of other canine chow merchants? Mr Hamel has now tried to answer this criticism in two ways: by setting up a new consultancy called Strategos, and by writing a new paper on the more practical question of how you go about generating strategies.*

Management focus

Although Mr Hamel admits that companies cannot generate innovative strategies on demand, he advocates three things to help successful strategy emerge:

- **More outsiders** Firms should invite new recruits, and those far away from the head office, to help set strategies. PECO Energy, a utility based in eastern Pennsylvania, has installed computer kiosks around the company to make it easier for employees to make suggestions on strategy.
  Mr Hamel recommends increasing the 'genetic variety' of the firm by recruiting people from a variety of backgrounds – as Microsoft did when it

---

* 'The Search for Strategy', Strategos Working Paper.

appointed Bob Bejan, a former dancer in Broadway's 'Chorus Line', to run its Internet Service.

- **New ways of thinking** Mr Hamel has long urged managers to think of companies as repositories of skills rather than portfolios of products. Sometimes a new perspective can be gained simply by flying to another country. Nokia, a Finnish telecoms company, sent a group of managers to Venice Beach in California and the King's Road in London to observe the way that mobile phones were becoming fashion accessories.

- **More passion** The more involved people are in making a strategy, the harder they will work to make it succeed. 'I don't just want something that gathers dust on my shelf,' says Glen Highland, boss of Data Card Corporation, a firm that makes the machines that make credit cards. 'I want something that engages my people.' Mr Hamel suggests bringing together a relatively small group of people, representing each level of the company, to focus on the problem. The boss plays the role of Oprah Winfrey, directing the microphone at the people who have the most interesting things to say.

The trouble with Oprah

A management technique that promises both to generate innovative strategies and mobilise workers' enthusiasm sounds a little too good to be true. Why should bringing more people into a discussion increase the number of really good ideas? As anybody who has attended a meeting knows, big groups can produce 'group think' rather than creativity.

Besides, many companies that have devised bold new strategies have been the opposite of democratic, depending on strong-willed individuals with a clear idea of where they want to take their businesses. Would Rupert Murdoch have been able to change the rules of the newspaper-publishing business in Britain in the mid-1980s if he had invited the print unions to discuss strategy? At Virgin, Richard Branson may be known for his convivial management style, but he relies on his own judgement for big strategic decisions, such as selling his music business to concentrate on airlines.

It is also extremely difficult for any successful organisation to obey Mr Hamel's injunction to acquire 'genetic diversity'. Indeed, they often invest heavily in selection and training to forge the company type: Andersen Consulting has its 'Androids' and Disney its 'clear-cut zealots'. Firms such as Procter & Gamble, General Electric and Motorola, which have promoted only from within, have performed better than Colgate, Westinghouse and Zenith, which have made a point of adding to their gene pool with outside recruits.

Similarly, many highly successful companies have no interest in engaging in lengthy strategy debates. McKinsey, for instance, has thrived by sticking to a simple policy: hire good people, offer them a rigorous training and then wait for clients to knock at the door. Andersen Consulting, which held a series of company-wide debates in the early 1990s, recently cancelled plans for a replay. If even consultancies treat strategy with suspicion, Mr Hamel has his work cut out.

(*Source:* The Economist, *1 March 1997*)

Discussion

The article proposes Porter's and Hamel's ideas as alternative schools of strategy, with Hamel's ideas at best difficult to implement and at worst, unrealistic. Alternative views they may be, but they should not be considered mutually exclusive. The Harvard Business Review articles which The Economist review discusses are of course far more sophisticated in the thinking and arguments presented than is summarised in Box 3.2. There, Porter (1996, reproduced in full in the Reader, Chapter 4) stressed his anxiety that managers are no longer distinguishing between operational effectiveness and strategy (a distinction that the Jollibee mini-case makes very clear) and that as a result, 'bit by bit, almost imperceptibly, management tools have taken the place of strategy' (p. 61). Porter argues that both are essential to superior performance (as in the airline mini-cases or the Red Cross reorganisation), but that they work in very different ways. In Porter's terms having a strategy means deliberately exercising choice: 'choosing a particular set of activities to deliver a unique mix of value'. He considers this to be the reason why Japanese corporations are becoming less successful in the 1990s. Their success was based predominantly on operational efficiency and their lead has been narrowed and in some sectors wiped out. Porter argues that they will now 'have to learn strategy', by which he means making hard choices about markets, customers, service levels, and so on. Imitating each other's improvements in quality, outsourcing or forming partnerships, leads to a convergence of strategies and 'a series of races down identical paths no one can win.' Continuous improvement in operational effectiveness alone is not the basis of advantage. Porter argues that choices and trade-offs are essential in strategy. It is important to choose and limit what an organisation offers. (Indeed, that is the central issue in the Airbus worked case accompanying this book. You are asked to choose on behalf of Airbus. Should it build the new large aircraft A3XX? From that strategic choice will follow all the decisions about how to restructure Airbus and make it most operationally effective. Operational effectiveness is critical but it is not a substitute for strategic thinking or a substitute for choosing a strategy.)

Hamel urges managers to think of organisations as 'repositories of skills rather than portfolios of products'. By contrast to Porter, his Harvard Business Review article (1996) is about how to create more imaginative strategies within organisations: 'to invite new voices into the strategy-making process, to encourage new perspectives, to start new conversations that span organisational boundaries, and then to help synthesise unconventional options into a point of view about corporate direction' (p. 82). Hamel is thus more concerned to enrich the strategy process, the way in which organisations can renovate their strategic thinking, while Porter is concerned that organisations should make strategic choices and then focus coherently on the consequences of that choice for the way the organisation is managed.

As usual with articles of this type, you should take a critical view of the perspectives presented.

3.5 SUMMARY

To summarise the purpose of our examples and discussions in this section, we may use Ghemawat and Ricart i Costa's (1993) ideas of static and dynamic efficiency and the organisational tension between the two. They define 'static efficiency' as 'a continuous search for improvements within a fixed set of initial (environmental and organisational) conditions', whereas 'dynamic efficiency' involves continuous reconsideration of initial conditions. They see the tension between static and dynamic efficiency as central to strategy. It is certainly at the heart of the debate in this section, and elsewhere in the course, on the wisdom of pursuing a targeted competitive position (static) as opposed to new visions of how to compete (dynamic); or pursuing fit with the organisation's existing resources, capabilities or strategy (static) compared with the pursuit of 'stretch' (dynamic).

4 SUSTAINABILITY

In Book 1 of this course you were told that strategy is about 'those actions which determine whether an organisation survives, prospers or dies'. Most organisations can manage to survive for a while, but what does it take to be around for decades and generations? That is the test of sustainability, and sustainability brings a sense of rigour to strategy.

In determining the contribution to sustainability of any source of advantage, organisations must determine whether:

1. the organisation has the capability to replicate and develop the distinctive resources and capabilities at the heart of its advantage
2. those distinctive resources and capabilities will provide unique benefits for customers which they will value
3. competitors are able to replicate or imitate the resources and capabilities involved, or to innovate in such a way as to negate any advantage from them.

The importance of preventing competitors from imitating sources of advantage helps explain why it is generally accepted that those resources that are difficult for competitors to identify or acquire are likely to be more sustainable as sources of advantage (remember the discussions on imitability and causal ambiguity in capability-building in Book 4, and corporate strategy synergy in Book 10). Very often, therefore, intangible assets, or assets which are information or knowledge-based and which cannot therefore be acquired easily, are more valuable to organisations because they are less imitable and more sustainable. For example, the biotechnology industry seeks its advantage in more efficient knowledge-based technologies that can be protected through legal patents.

> [Biotechnology] can increase yields and productivity by substituting information for stuff. That's critical. Biotechnology is essentially a subset of information technology, because it is about DNA-encoded information. Putting the right information in the genes of a plant, for example, enables the plant to repel or destroy insect pests. We don't have to spray the plant with pesticides – with stuff. When growers spray crops today, up to 90 per cent becomes waste. Very little of it gets to its target. Most of it ends up on the soil. The right information in the plant means less stuff is wasted.
>
> *(Shapiro, 1996, p. 13)*

There has, of course, been much public debate over the wisdom and ethics of such 'genetic engineering' of human foods. Shapiro is CEO of Monsanto, one of the companies pursuing the commercial opportunities of biotechnology most forcefully, and he puts the economic case for biotechnologically modified foods. A less controversial example of the economic value that knowledge-based assets and learning can create is given in the example in Box 4.1. In this example, Stewart argues that knowledge-based innovations have helped the manufacturers of aluminium cans to reduce significantly the input costs of their physical raw materials, and render the competing steel can obsolete.

BOX 4.1

Consider a beer can. Open it if you want, but consider the can. If it is symbolic of anything, it is an emblem of blue-collar industrial work, an everyday accessory for 'Joe Six-Pack', union member, factory worker, but it is far more: it is an artifact of a new, knowledge-based economy, evidence of how knowledge has become the most important component of business activity. To see how this is so is to begin to understand an extraordinary transformation, the emergence of the Information Age.

Three decades ago, that can would probably have been steel. Aluminum companies have always wanted to replace steel wherever it is used; indeed, they have long been imbued with an almost missionary zeal to peddle the metal, which was considered a miraculous substance when it was introduced to the public at an international exposition in Paris in 1855. Although aluminum is the most common metallic element in the earth's crust, refining it was outrageously expensive, requiring costly chemicals or even more costly electric power from batteries. In the nineteenth century, aluminum cost so much that King Christian X of Denmark ordered up an aluminum crown and France's conspicuously consuming Emperor Napoleon III had a dinner service made of it, which he used for guests who deserved something fancier than mere gold. Not till electricity became plentiful and cheap did aluminum find much of a commercial market. (Electricity remains the single largest cost in making aluminum.) By the 1950s, steel's lucrative can-making business had become an obvious target, but not an easy one to hit. Even with cheap power, aluminum costs more than steel; breweries and soft-drink bottlers weren't about to switch to a pricier material for a mere container. But aluminum is also easier to work than steel, and in that fact the industry found its chance: steel's price advantage could be overcome if the industry could exploit aluminum's malleability to manufacture a can that used less metal than steel cans required. In 1958, the Adolph Coors Company developed a seven-ounce aluminum can, first used by a small Hawaiian brewery, but the process did not lend itself to mass production. Five years later, Reynolds Metals invented a way to mass-produce a twelve-ounce can. ... Within four years, Coca-Cola and Pepsi-Cola began using aluminum cans; today, the steel beverage can is almost nonexistent in the United States – steel's market share is about 1 percent – and it is losing ground in international markets.

That first aluminum can represented a triumph of know-how over nature. Weighing just .66 of an ounce, about half what a steel can weighed, the aluminum container substituted knowledge – years of research – for raw material. Since then, improvements in manufacturing processes, subtle changes in the alloys used to make can sheet, and other brainpower investments have steadily reduced the amount of metal in a can. Today, empty, your beer can weighs just .48 of an ounce, about three fourths as much as Reynolds's first can. The can contains less material and more science. The beer may have a head, but the can is about 25 percent knowledge.

One of the world's largest factories making can sheet stands in Alcoa, Tennessee, a town built in the 1930s by the giant aluminum maker; Alcoa put it there to get an inexpensive hydroelectric power from the Tennessee River. The factory originally made dozens of products – even aluminum phonograph records; now it makes only ingot and, from the ingot, can sheet. In the factory, huge bars of gleaming metal – 74 inches wide, 21 inches thick, 20 feet long, each weighing 35,000 pounds – pass through a series of rolling mills until they have been flattened to a thickness of about one one-

> hundredth of an inch, the same as a couple of sheets of paper. The 20-foot ingot becomes a sheet more than 3,000 feet long; and over all that length the metal varies in thickness by no more than one *ten-thousandth* of an inch.
>
> Now, having squeezed and rolled raw material out of their product, aluminum makers are going after its other major physical ingredient, electricity: can sheet made with melted, recycled metal uses only 5 percent of the electricity needed to make ingot from scratch, which explains why about two out of three aluminum cans are recycled. It still holds twelve ounces of beer, but the can itself contains dramatically less material and energy – and more brains.
>
> Finish your beer. Pick up the can. You can crush it with one hand. Yet when it's full, that same can is strong enough to be stacked in towers six feet high on the floor of a supermarket, piled in the back of a delivery truck, jounced over potholed roads, slammed around and dropped by delivery crews, chilled in a 35-degree refrigerator, or baked in 95-degree sun. What holds it up? Not the metal – crushing it shows that. No, what keeps the can rigid, strong enough to withstand pressure of up to ninety pounds per square inch, is the gas inside: carbon dioxide bubbles in a Bud or a Coke, a shot of nitrogen in a can of tomato juice. Less metal – less energy – held up by something you can neither see nor feel: Joe Six-Pack's Industrial Age talisman has become an icon of the Knowledge Age, the economy of the intangible.
>
> (Stewart, 1997, pp. 3–5)

In the biotechnology example, Shapiro suggests that more precise knowledge leads to more effective use of resources. Stewart's description of beer can competition is also an example of knowledge replacing 'stuff'. Knowledge can thus be a strategic asset and one for which there is less risk of imitation than tangible assets. However, there may be high or higher risk of loss of knowledge-based assets where the key resources and capabilities in question are those of skilled individuals. It is hard to build sustainable long-term advantage where no long-term claim to the loyalty of those individuals can be established. For example, in the mid-1990s Deutsche Bank – with a long history of successful German commercial banking – started to pursue a strategy to remake itself as a global investment bank capable of competing with the large American and Japanese banks. It moved its global investment headquarters to London under the Deutsche Morgan Grenfell brand and expanded aggressively by hiring key staff from competitors (600 in North America alone in 1996) and by lowering fees. DMG was widely believed to be competing at a loss, however, due to the massive salary costs of this rapid recruitment expansion, reflecting the job mobility that key professionals in this industry enjoy. The rapid expansion also resulted in some failure of the internal systems of control and governance, with a costly and embarrassing investment scandal, surfacing in one of DMG's star European investment funds in 1996.

Thus, the resources and capabilities that form the source of advantage need to be appropriated by the organisation, rather than the individual employees involved. This can occur where key capabilities are created through the clustering of resources, such as can be found in professional teams. This clustering of resources or assets in unique combinations has also been the focus of much of the growth in the use of alliances, networks and joint ventures to pursue strategies internationally or in new or 'converging' industries (such as 'The Information Superhighway', the nexus of competing technologies featured in the course video accompanying Book 10).

Activity 4.1

All these issues of sustainable sources of advantage are addressed in the final video, 'Dynamic Strategy', based on the strategy of the global fast food chain Hard Rock Café and its parent company the Rank Organisation. Hard Rock has been successful for 25 years and the video looks at its chances of survival for the next 25 years. While watching the video please consider the following questions:

How would you define Hard Rock's strategy?

What has contributed to Hard Rock's success in the last 25 years?

Is the Hard Rock strategy sustainable?

Has the corporate strategy of Rank (Hard Rock's parent company) had any impact on Hard Rock's competitive strategy?

You should now watch the video (VC 0865, band 2) 'Dynamic Strategy', featuring Hard Rock Café.

Discussion

We will discuss these questions drawing on the interviews and discussion with managers and staff at Hard Rock and executives at Rank, some of whom appear in the video.

Strategy at Hard Rock has often been implicit rather than explicit, emergent rather than deliberate. The central Hard Rock concept is its association with rock music, the rock memorabilia which forms the decor of the cafés, and the associated merchandising. To quote Andrew Teare (CEO of Rank): 'It seemed quite clear to me that we had very quickly to take it back to its music roots, because its roots in rock music was really the thing that had given it the legs to go for twenty five years.'

Hard Rock's success has depended heavily on managing the 'intangibles' of a service business providing a certain type of experience for the customer (see Book 11, Section 4.3.1). It has been especially successful at motivating its front-line staff. In a sector characterised by high labour turnover Hard Rock inspires tremendous loyalty; in 1996 (their 25th year) the London restaurant gave 25 awards to staff with ten or more years' service and three awards for 25 years' service. As Teare says: 'You can't imitate that. You have to create it and work at it.' It has unique ways of perpetuating the corporate culture as it continues its expansion around the world. The roving ambassador Rita Gilligan ('our Director of Attitude'), one of the original Hard Rock waitresses from its opening in 1972, describes the culture of the business to new recruits around the world. These are all durable resources and capabilities which are hard to imitate and difficult to substitute. They are therefore precisely the kind of assets that contribute to sustainability despite increasing numbers of copycat 'theme restaurant' competitors.

After Andrew Teare at Rank took over, many of the changes he made were beneficial to Hard Rock. He restructured all Rank's operating divisions and as part of that restructuring created Hard Rock as a single division: 'Hard Rock needed real profile within the business so that we could drive that business very much harder.' He set out to find (and subsequently appointed) a Chief Executive with a music industry background to run and develop Hard Rock worldwide. He saw in Hard Rock, Rank's 'clearest global brand capable of a very grand scale of development'. He negotiated to unite the two halves of Hard Rock which 'put us in control of a global brand, which is about the twenty-fifth best recognised brand in the world'. International expansion means recruiting local people, but they put alongside them people who know the Hard Rock culture and how best to adapt it to new locations. Strict central reporting structures are maintained, yet it remains a very flat organisation, run by individual café managers at the local level.

Hard Rock cannot be guaranteed another successful 25 years, but a brief review of their strategy, structure, culture and systems, combined with some unique mechanisms for internal learning, suggest a clear strategic intent, distinctive assets and some non-imitable resources which may provide a strong basis for survival in the volatile sector they originally helped to create.

4.1 STRATEGY AND COMMITMENT

At the heart of strategy is the need to define the purpose of the enterprise and to turn ideas into sustained action through the imagination and energy of people at all levels in the organisation. Purpose cannot be defined solely in terms of financial targets. Few employees rush into work each day eager to make money for remote shareholders. Strategy has to be made more immediate and more tangible to people's working reality, as was vividly illustrated in the 'Dynamic Strategy' video for Hard Rock Café and its culture, values and commitment.

In the 1980s, the dominant models of strategy were based on industrial economics and emphasised the importance of industry structure, position within an industry and selection by managers of a favourable industry segment. Innovative strategies based on capability depend greatly on the internal mechanisms of information and co-ordination in companies. Since this requires commitment to building capabilities over the long term, strategy becomes a process of stretching and developing resources to meet a clear but evolving set of purposes. This takes strategic management beyond the analytical approaches such as Porter's 'five forces' with which we began, with strategy to be chosen so as to 'fit' the market. Instead, like Konosuke Matsushita or Bill Gates, great entrepreneurs do not base strategy on today's resources but on a belief that they can create new ones faster than competitors. As well as a battle of resources, competition has also become a battle around the quality of strategic thinking and competing strategies. In example after example we have shown how management skill and commitment can make the difference between success or gradual (and sometimes spectacular) failure.

5 Summary and conclusion

Clarity about strategic issues and strategic choices for your organisation matters. All organisations have strategic alternatives open to them, so how are we to deal with the complexity attached to every managerial or business decision? In this course we have presented strategy as an outcome of the interrelationship of industry characteristics, strategic flexibility and organisational capabilities. That relationship holds for all organisations whether product or service, national and local government, small, medium-sized or multinational enterprises, commercial or not-for-profit. The fact that organisations such as Honda, Hard Rock or the Red Cross are very different does not matter. The concepts to which you have been introduced in this course are transferable across them all. Your learning here acts as a potential economy of scope for you – a resource which may be used in many different contexts to achieve a variety of purposes from the same single investment of your time and effort.

We have not been greatly concerned in this course about discussing how difficult it is to make strategic decisions in turbulent environments. We have simply assumed this in our approach throughout. We have spoken instead of static and dynamic approaches to strategic thinking and strategic decision-making and of their contribution to the sustainability of strategies, and the organisations which pursue those strategies, over the long term.

Echoing Hamel and Prahalad (1996), we assume that while many traditional industry boundaries are breaking down or becoming 'fuzzy', existing corporations still have to create viable strategies for an uncertain future within unclear industry frameworks. We assume that control of resources often depends on alliances with others outside your own organisational or geographic boundaries, so that issues of control tend to involve alliance-building, coalition-management and co-ordination. We assume that flexible learning organisations depend upon the motivation and commitment of knowledge-workers, while at the same time operational efficiency may require them to be outsourced. Strategic innovation often requires cross-functional, interdisciplinary collaboration across boundaries in organisations whose managers are still often more comfortable with hierarchies or multidivisional matrix structures.

We have used the vocabulary and generally accepted the principle of the resource-based approach to strategy. We have used it to explain heterogeneity: why organisations within the same industry or sector differ. It tells us that this is because clusters of resources differ between organisations in the same industry. It tells us that corporate strategy involves identifying resources and building and leveraging such competences across business units. It tells us that strategy for all large organisations, including multinationals, is about managing tensions between integration and co-ordination, centralisation and decentralisation, to find the optimal configuration of resources to achieve strategic objectives. To the extent that this is true, competition to acquire resources and to use them most effectively is at the heart of strategy.

We have been revisiting basic ideas about what strategy is for and what is meant when an issue is called 'strategic'. We have warned against an over-reliance on strategic recipes. Such recipes dominate, stagnate, create opportunities for innovation and are then in turn replaced. Over the longer term, and sometimes in the short term, all sources of advantage must be challenged.

We must close by once again distinguishing between operational effectiveness and strategy. Each needs the other and *both* are essential to superior performance. We have attempted in this course to illustrate that fundamental point many times over. Finally, let us be clear that models and frameworks do not make strategy. Strategy is made by people exercising their judgement and making choices.

REFERENCES

Bettis, R.A. and Prahalad, C.K. (1995) 'The dominant logic: retrospective and extension', *Strategic Management Journal*, Vol. 16, pp. 5–14.

Ghemawat, P. and Ricart i Costa, J.E. (1993) 'The organisational tension between static and dynamic efficiency', *Strategic Management Journal*, Vol. 14, pp. 59–73.

Hamel, G. (1996) 'Strategy as revolution', *Harvard Business Review*, July/August, pp. 69–82.

Hamel, G. and Prahalad, C.K. (1996) 'Competing in the new economy: managing out of bounds', *Strategic Management Journal*, Vol. 17, pp. 237–42.

Porter, M.E. (1996) 'What is strategy?', *Harvard Business Review*, November/December, pp. 61–78.

Rumelt, R.P., Schendel, D.E. and Teece, D.J. (1994) 'Fundamental issues in strategy' in Rumelt, R.P., Schendel, D.E. and Teece, D.J. (eds) *Fundamental Issues in Strategy*, Harvard Business School Press, Boston, MA.

Shapiro, R. (1996) 'A new model of growth', in *Strategy*, No. 10.

Stewart, T.A. (1997) *Intellectual Capital: the new wealth of organizations*, Nicholas Brealey Publishing, London.

Acknowledgements

Grateful acknowledgement is made to the following sources for permission to reproduce material in this book:

Text

Box 3.1: Warman, J. 1997, 'Charity given a facelift', *The Guardian*, 18 January 1997; *Box 3.2:* 'Making strategy', *The Economist*, 1 March 1997, © 1997 Economist Newspapers Limited, *Box 4.1:* Stewart, T.A. (1997) *Intellectual Capital: the new wealth of organizations*, Nicholas Brearley Publishing Ltd.

Figure

Figure 3.1: Courtesy of *Private Eye*.